GW00983058

DAILY

FINANCE
for life

HOW THE INTELLIGENT FINANCE PLAN COULD WORK FOR YOU.

The Intelligent Finance plan can offer you a mortgage, savings, personal loan, current account and credit card. Like all good ideas, ours is very simple.
We connect the money you have with the money you borrow, in any product combination that suits you, to make you better off.

HERE'S A COUPLE OF EXAMPLES.

You could **choose to pay no interest** on part of your mortgage. So how does that work? Well, say you normally have £2,000 in your current account and a mortgage of £50,000. If they were with Intelligent Finance, you could choose to receive no interest on the £2,000 in your current account and pay no interest on £2,000 of your mortgage. And because Intelligent Finance doesn't reduce the amount you pay each month, you'll pay off your mortgage quicker.

Or you could **choose to earn higher rates of interest** on your savings. Here's how. If you had £2,000 in savings and a £4,000 personal loan, with Intelligent Finance you could connect them together to earn the personal loan rate of interest on the amount in your savings which is equal to the amount remaining on your loan. You would still make your monthly payments on the outstanding balance of your loan, but your savings would be working so much harder.

IT COULDN'T BE EASIER TO OPEN A PLAN.

For further information or to apply for Intelligent Finance products call 0845 606 4343 or visit www.if.com.

DAILY⚔EXPRESS

FINANCE
for life

a guide to money management for modern lifestyles

edited by steve lodge

Chelsea Financial Services

KOGAN
PAGE

Acknowledgements

With thanks for technical advice to Philippa Gee and Tom McPhail of independent financial adviser Torquil Clark (0800 413186; www.tqonline.co.uk).

Original copy by Tony Levene.

Publisher's note

First published in 2002

Kogan Page Ltd
120 Pentonville Road
London N1 9JN
www.kogan-page.co.uk

THE EXPRESS

© Express Newspapers 2002

British Library Cataloguing in Publication Data

A CIP record for this book is available from the British Library

ISBN 0 7494 3554 2

Typeset by Saxon Graphics Ltd, Derby
Printed and bound in Great Britain by Thanet Press Ltd, Margate, Kent

Financial Planning
Who needs it?

The answer, almost certainly, is 'You do'.

From cradle to grave, we consistently need the services available through Independent Financial Advisers (IFAs).

When we pick an adviser, be it solicitor, accountant, health specialist, etc, we want a high quality customer service (eg. prompt, reliable, respectful) which adds tangible value (eg. a saving in tax, satisfactory settlement of a dispute, relief from a troublesome ache or pain).

Certainly there are many financial advisers who can readily deliver on service, but just how can they add value?

Let's take mortgages for instance. Did you know tax and mortgage costs can account for around 50% of an individual's earned lifetime income? The savings an independent adviser could achieve here could easily fund a world cruise or two.

The arrival of a baby into the family creates the need to review the level and type of protection afforded to parents or guardians in the event of their ill health, serious accident, and yes, even death. Any surviving partner will vouch for the this!

As "baby" grows, school and university fees and possibly marriage arrangements require thoughtful, long term planning and funding(on the bright side, no wedding means another world cruise!)

From the outset of one's working life, plans for protecting income, for pensions and other future provisions should give us pause for thought. Pensions legislation is a moveable feast, as evidenced by the recent introduction of Stakeholder plans. Regular reviews by an adviser (one legally responsible for representing your interest rather than those of a particular product provider), is an essential investment of time for those of us unfamiliar with the complexities of the world of pensions. Selecting the right rather than "wrong" provider will have a significant impact on the value of your pension fund when you come to claim benefits.

While pension provision will hopefully meet your day-to-day retirement requirements, other investment vehicles such as ISAs, Unit Trusts, With Profit Bonds, National Savings Certificates, etc. are a necessity to fund capital needs for larger expenditure items such as holidays, home improvements, car replacements, etc. Many older people get trapped in cash poor, asset rich positions. Independent advice on safe equity release schemes could make a real difference to their quality of life without increasing expenditure or risking premature foreclosure.

Increases in property prices and investment returns have pushed many estates beyond the nil band threshold for Inheritance Tax purposes. This is yet another area where independent advice on how not to bequeath money to the Inland Revenue could add significant value to the wealth and well-being of your immediate family.

Similar to the need for Inheritance Tax planning, the potential burdens of long term care also arise from the shift to lengthier, but not always fitter, lives. Once again, the professional and friendly service of an IFA could add substantial benefit to you and those you care about.

The old cliché "fail to plan; plan to fail" encompasses the real reason for obtaining advice from a fully qualified IFA. Every stage of our journey through Shakespeare's "seven ages of man" highlights the need for and benefits of financial planning. Nearly all IFAs offer an initial consultation free of charge – it could be the most profitable half-hour of your life.

Ashley Law is one of many IFA firms, however, it has the unique distinction that each of its "Branch Managers" has personally invested in the Company, thus clients have the security of a large company and personal service locally offered by independent financial advisers. With over 70 outlets Ashley Law is ideally positioned to assist clients.

For more information on Ashley Law visit
www.ashleylaw.co.uk or call: 0500 104 106 Free

Contents

Introduction

If the title of this book – *Finance for Life* – sounds like that of a self-help publication then that is probably no bad thing. Never mind how hard money can be to come by, looking after it has become ever more complicated in recent years. We are all expected to make so many choices for our personal finances, from mortgages to investments to pensions. Gone, it seems, are the days of one simple solution. The Government appears to want to provide less and less as of right, in terms of pensions and healthcare. At the same time working lives have become both more flexible and insecure.

This makes looking after the money you have all the more important. The difference that good or bad money management can make to your overall finances is potentially huge. Importantly, too, no one is going to do it all for you. The world of finance is a jungle where you are on your own. You have to take care of yourself and your family if you have one. What about the professionals – the banks, the building societies, the insurance companies, the fund managers, the brokers, and the independent financial advisers (IFAs)? Don't they have the necessary expertise? Some have it aplenty. Some have just enough to scrape into a job. But the last two decades of financial 'advice' have all too often benefited the professionals at the expense of other people. A quick website trawl through newspaper archives will throw up a huge number of matches between 'mis-selling' and 'personal pensions', between 'technology funds' and 'massive losses', and between 'endowments' and 'mortgage shortfalls'. The professionals' first duty is to themselves. They need you to produce their commission and other earnings. Equally, you need them to access and process the world of finance, whether face to face, on the phone or via the Internet. They are not all rogues. But there are enough unscrupulous salespeople, low quality products and bad value deals around for the unwary to be caught out or lose out.

This book offers a map to the world of money. It provides a guide so that, at the very least, you will be suspicious of the rip-off merchants who still seem to thrive despite a whole raft of regulations and the activities of the watchdog Financial Services Authority. The book does not assume, as do so many financial company adverts, leaflets and attitudes, that we all live with our 2.4 children in married bliss in a three-bedroom semi in the suburbs. Many of us do, and there is nothing wrong with that. But it is now a minority arrangement.

This book considers lifestyles, life stages and life activities. Men, women, young, old, married, single, straight, gay, should all find information and tips in the following chapters.

Working for It looks at what to do with the money that comes in. It describes how to take control of your income, prevent your loans and credit card bills taking over your life, and budgeting for a better tomorrow.

Health and Wealth is about how to make sure a sudden catastrophe does not take it all away. It is also about getting best value from insurance companies, which would like you to put all your money into their policies.

Making It Work for You is how to ensure that your spare money is best used. It is split into two sections; savings and investment.

Money and Property describes how to save up for, and buy a home. It is a guide through the mortgage maze.

Household Finances is about the choices we have in family formation, whether to get married or not (where we have that option), paying for children, and in splitting up or divorcing.

Retirement sets out a five-age viewpoint on saving up for those years when you finally stop working. It has information on the various forms of pension – and describes what to do if, like most people, your pension planning has fallen behind.

Inheriting It, Leaving It combines those two great inevitabilities – death and taxes. It looks at inheritances, wills, and, finally, funerals.

Even if you pick up one idea that makes you more money than the 'advice' from the professionals or stops you losing your cash, both your purchase of *Finance for Life* and the writing of it will have been worthwhile.

1

Working for It

Budgeting and managing your finances

Financial companies all too often assume a 'normal' work and lifestyle pattern. With many advisers and the firms they work for still believing that the country consists of married couples with 2.4 children, where the man works and the woman either stays at home or is a subsidiary earner, it is no surprise that millions feel alienated.

Add to that half-a-century-old picture the expectation that parents want to save for private education, that you will want to retire at a fixed future date, and that you intend buying your home over the traditional 25 years and it is easy to see why financial planning for the future is off the agenda for so many.

Life is not like that any more – even if it ever was. We all start off with what we earn either from work, investments and savings or pensions. After that, we have choices, many of which concern financial companies. Financial planning should not be about shoe-horning your life into a stereotype. Whether you sort out your own money on a DIY basis or pay for help, start out with as clear an idea as possible of your future needs and future earning capacity. Then insist that any adviser you talk to takes heed.

Gay or straight, young or old, male or female, in a relationship or out of a relationship, the first essential of money management is to ask yourself 'Does anyone else depend on me financially?' If there are dependents – or there might be some in the foreseeable future – your financial planning will be different than if you have no one else to worry about.

Those with no worries about other people can afford to spend more or save more, do not need to concern themselves greatly with life insurance as there might be no one to inherit the money, and can take chances with investments knowing that no one other than themselves will be hurt if the strategy unravels. Those in this position include not just the long-term single but also those with partners who can stand on their own financial feet and parents whose children have long since grown up.

By contrast, those with responsibilities have to manage money with a permanently nagging doubt. 'What if ...?' has to be the first thought before any cash management action.

Whatever age you are and lifestyle you espouse, start off with working out your future earnings pattern and the implications. This could include:

- Self employment or contract work – this is increasingly popular especially where you have an in-demand skill such as plumbing or information technology. Here your earnings pattern will be characterised by big ups and downs. Over a year, you may well earn more than someone who is employed but the chances are you will have periods when no money is coming in – holiday time if at no other – and cash flow difficulties when customers are slow in paying. This pattern will determine your financial planning – as far as possible you will need to avoid anything with a regular commitment in favour of paying bigger amounts on the occasions when you have funds. Your earnings are unlikely to progress – once you have fully mastered a skill, that is as far as you will probably get.

- Work with periods off. Whether this is because you are in a job with a higher risk of substantial periods of unemployment or you decide you want to take time off every few years, your main need will be to budget for non-earning time. Savings are important to tide you over but so, too, is the need to apply for any credit you want during times in employment. No matter how well you cope with non-earning periods, home loan and credit card companies will be much less willing to deal with you when you are not working. However, they cannot generally take borrowing facilities away from you providing you are keeping up payments no matter how many status or job changes you have.

- Retirement – many older people are juggling money from several sources such as the state pension, one or more occupational pensions, personal pensions and income from capital saved. Because people in this group tend to have more put by, they are a prime target for financial salespeople. Recent financial problems at pension firm Equitable Life underline the importance of spreading your money around and not putting every egg in one basket. You have choices, which are enhanced by the fact that you will probably have paid off your mortgage. These range from spending very little and leaving it all to children and grandchildren to spending all your money and then relying on the state.

- Regular employment – you earn roughly the same, month in and month out. Provided the job is secure, your financial planning should be relatively easy – you certainly have plenty of choices.

- Regular salary with bonuses, overtime or commission payments. If your needs are covered by your basic salary, you are fortunate. But you may find that your basic is not enough to live on and that you are reliant on the extras. If so, your earnings pattern might be more akin to someone with self-employment or contract work. Lenders will want to know how regular the extras are and whether they can be relied upon in the future. One idea would be to see how much you really need each month and save any additional amounts for poor earning periods.

- Regular salary with annual increments or frequent promotions. This is a good position to be in but watch out for financial advisers who will assume too much in the way of wage increases for the future – and lenders who ignore your future potential.

Whatever your earnings pattern – weekly pay packet or the odd large sum from time to time – your spending is likely to be more regular. The typical person pays food bills weekly, mortgage and phone bills monthly, gas and electricity monthly or three-monthly, insurances annually and so on.

Working out how much you spend over a typical three month period could be a first step to sorting out your money. It could also identify areas where you could cut back spending without too much hardship. Make a list of your outgoings – old bank and credit card statements will help with larger sums such as holidays or Christmas spending.

Knowing your expenditure may not make you feel good. And always add 10 per cent to your spending as a safety net to cover all the items that are forgotten about. Without a personal budget, your financial planning will be at best haphazard and at worst chaotic.

For most people, the difference between keeping their head above water or starting to sink under debt lies in how they look after and spend their money. Most of us can list our main expenditure items but we forget (or push to the back of our minds) all the smaller things and little luxuries that are fine if we can afford them, but are unnecessary purchases if finances are already stretched. Opposite you will find a list of items that make up common spending patterns. Every individual is different – so ignore pet care if you have no animals at home, childcare if you have no children and so on.

Now compare this spending with your take home pay. This is easy to calculate from your last pay packet if you have a job. But if you are self-employed or have an irregular work pattern, work back to a weekly or monthly figure from your last annual after-tax earnings figure. If you have ups and downs in your spending, aim at calculating a monthly or weekly amount from the annual sum, which should take care of high and low-paying months or weeks.

The two figures are unlikely to balance. You will be left with money over, which you can save, or with a deficit that will need to be paid for with credit. Living within your means and saving is obviously preferable but many will not be able to afford to do this all the time. But

Outgoings – Checklist

Bank
Credit card interest and fees
Overdraft interest
Monthly service charge
Personal loan servicing
Mortgage
Household
Rent
Council Tax
Home insurance
Cleaning
Gardening
Furnishings
Utilities
Gas
Water
Electricity
Fixed line phone
Mobile phone
Internet charges
Car
Insurance
Petrol/diesel
Car tax (vehicle excise duty)
Maintenance
Replacement fund
Road rescue subscription
Cleaning
Childcare
Clothes
School fees
Fees for out-of-school activities
Information
Books
Magazines
Newspapers
TV licence
Evening class tuition
Leisure and entertainment
Satellite/cable TV subscription
Health club fees
Cinema/theatre
Video rentals

Sports goods
Sports tickets
Games
CDs, DVDs, tapes
Eating out
Pubs
Cafes
Workplace canteen
Sandwich bar
Snacks (chocolate bars, crisps,
soft drinks)
Restaurants
Gifts
Birthday
Christmas
Other
Treats for self
Clothing
Outerwear
Underwear
Shoes
Dry cleaning/repairs
Groceries
Healthcare
Life insurance
Medical insurance
Dental costs
Optician's bill
Medicines
Holidays
Travel
Food
Accommodation
Insurance
Travel
Public transport to work
Public transport for leisure activities
Bicycle
Pets
Food
Vets' bills
Housing and other costs

borrowing does not necessarily mean you should not save. Borrowing within limits and with controls is all part of living within your means. Big long-term loans such as mortgages can be part of a budget – call it 'rent' or 'accommodation expenses' if you prefer – but don't forget you cannot walk away like a tenant.

Being disciplined over money matters can reduce borrowing costs and increase returns on savings. Some homebuyers now opt for all-in-one banking, savings and borrowing packages. These can work just as the banks that provide them say they do – provided you run them rather than they control you.

Money and control are inseparable. As political psychologist Dr Valerie Wilson says in *The Secret Life of Money* (Allen & Unwin 1999):

> 'When one's money feels out of control, one's life can feel out of control and vice versa. Controlling money coming in and controlling money going out involves constant readjustment and balancing. Controlling oneself (or not) is the key…from everyday management of cash to weekly budgeting, to spending and savings patterns, to relationships with financial institutions.'

Put on a personal level, it is estimated that one in three domestic disputes is directly driven by money, and many of the others are indirectly down to cash difficulties. The most difficult part of controlling money is managing debt.

Managing debt

Whether you are a high earner or just scraping by, there may never seem to be enough money to go around. But there is always someone around with a loan, whether it is a top City bank offering a million or two for a mortgage or a loan shark lending £20 to tide you over the next day or two.

There is nothing wrong with debt. It makes the economy go around. Equally, while debt is a good servant, it makes a bad master. There are some basic rules to follow:

- No one has a right to debt. Banks and building societies cannot be forced to lend to you.
- Banks and other lenders queue up to lend to those who are already well off.
- The poor may be charged higher interest rates than the rich.
- The more credit facilities you have, often the easier it is to gain an even greater amount.

Applying for a loan can be tricky – or very easy if you are willing to pay high interest rates. Whether an application is successful depends on your 'creditworthiness' and no two lenders use exactly the same criteria. Most start off by looking at your credit record obtained from information providers such as Equifax or Experian.

The data they supply is only as good as the information they receive. This will not include all your financial history but will concentrate on credit card and other debt. It will not show what goes on in your bank account or any savings accounts or investments you may have.

Lenders want the secure feeling of dealing with someone who has a background of 'reliability'. They will 'score' you on certain criteria including:

- presence on the electoral register – if you are not there, they may well turn you down;
- time you have spent with one employer – this discriminates against those with temporary jobs or who have just started out. It can also be difficult for the self-employed and others who run their own firm;
- how long you have lived in your present home – again, lenders do not like people who move a lot as they consider them 'unreliable';
- any previous defaults and arrears on debt repayments;
- county court judgements (CCJs);
- how many times you have applied for credit – if you keep on asking and receiving refusals, or if you have already collected enough credit from various sources to go very heavily into debt, lenders may say no. But, they also dislike those with no debt record at all;

- your age – being very young (you must be over 18) or very old could count against you;
- your salary – a low figure will not necessarily bring a refusal as some card issuers and other lenders will be prepared to offer a credit limit in line with your ability to repay;
- your relationship status – card companies are not supposed to discriminate against women with home responsibilities but effectively do so because these women cannot generally claim to have high earnings. People who are divorced with maintenance payments to make, especially if they are also involved in a subsequent relationship, are likely to be marked down on affordability grounds. And gay men who may think the pink pound is worth more as they generally have no dependants should think again. In fact, credit scorers often equate children and dependent partners as a source of financial stability and that can count for more than their cost.

Credit companies say that refusing credit to someone who cannot repay it is doing them a favour by keeping them out of debt problems. But if you are turned down, ask why. Lenders are under no obligation to tell you – some will, however. And others might take a second look at your record and conclude you are suitable after all. Most credit scoring is either automatic or carried out by junior employees so creating a fuss can help.

The best – and worst – ways to borrow money

Few households or individuals have strong enough cashflow to cope with making all their major purchases out of income or savings. So identifying the pluses and pitfalls of various ways of borrowing is essential to avoid paying over the odds or debt disasters. If you have spare savings beyond your emergency fund, use them. The interest paid on savings is rarely high and normally taxed. The interest charged on loans is generally anything from twice to twenty times the return on your savings.

Borrowers should always work out first how much they need, whether they require flexibility in repayments and how long they will take to pay it back. Never borrow for longer periods than you need. A five-year car loan when you intend replacing it after four years with a new model does not make financial sense.

Short term finance to cover a cash emergency – or a few days each month when your outgoings have exceeded your previous salary payment and you are waiting for the next – is best financed by an authorised overdraft from your bank. This means you have to sort out an arrangement with the bank before you use it – unauthorised overdrafts come with a panoply of ultra high interest charges and fixed penalties whose impact is disproportionally high on those who are the least in the red.

Banks vary greatly in how they charge for authorised overdrafts. Look out for:

- interest rates – some high street banks charge twice as much as others. Most banks quote rates as 'EARs' – the equivalent annual rate – but do not include fixed fees in their calculation;
- interest free overdraft buffers – some banks ignore the first £100 to £250 in the red;
- arrangement fees – you could pay as much as 2 per cent of the overdraft you might need or a flat £25;
- usage fees – some charge a fixed monthly fee every time you use the overdraft, even if it is just for a short time.

Credit cards are a good idea for smaller sums that you can afford to pay off quickly. There are over 200 credit cards on the market, although much of this choice is simply the same card repackaged with different labels.

Credit card users split into three main categories. Around two out of five always pay off their bill on time and never incur interest charges. They use the card purely as a convenient way of spending, or for purchases by post, phone or Internet. Those with this degree of discipline or financial muscle can afford to ignore the interest rate charged, but not the annual fees still imposed by some bank cards. Some cards offer bonuses based on spending, either as cashbacks, gifts from a catalogue, or contributions to a charity. These tend to give you back up to around one per cent of what you spend.

One in three card-holders are 'occasional' borrowers. They usually pay off their bills in full but do not do so on two or three occasions a year, typically holidays and Christmas. They should look for a low interest rate. But often the difference between paying off the entire balance and leaving some to the following month can depend on the 'interest free period'. Banks and other issuers like to claim this is anywhere between 46 and 56 days, depending on the card. But this apparently generous time period is a maximum – counted from the first possible purchase day in the card charging period of one calendar month.

The reality is that by the time you receive the bill by second class post, you could have seven to 17 days in which to settle up. And some four of these days will be needed to either clear your cheque or to ensure the payment has been received by post. However, some issuers, usually high street banks, allow payments by debit cards up to the midnight on the last day permitted. Most card issuers now charge £15 to £20 as a fixed rate penalty, as well as interest, if the minimum payment is not made by the final day each month.

The remaining one in four card-holders never clear their borrowings. They can adopt two tactics to keep costs down. One is to apply for a card that offers a low – or no – interest rate on balance transfers. These are known as 'introductory rates'. They usually last for six months but some can be longer – indefinite in a few cases. This is intended as a 'come-on' and if borrowers limit their use of the card to the transfer, they can reduce costs. They should not use the new card for fresh spending as this is generally expensive.

The second tactic is to look for a card that is designed for those who never clear their borrowings. This will have no interest free period but a lower interest rate.

Credit card borrowing is not normally cheap and some issuers have special cards with higher interest rates aimed at those with poor credit records.

Many stores offer their own cards. These usually have very high interest rates – there are a few exceptions including John Lewis and Fortnum & Mason. Their main attraction is the discounts some cards give on in-store purchases. They do, however, offer interest-free periods and can be transferred to a lower rate credit card.

Some stores offer 'interest-free' credit deals. But these are often on goods such as furniture where it is difficult to compare one store's products with another. Interest-free deals can therefore be for overpriced goods. And they usually come with strict penalties – be a day late with a payment and the entire purchase reverts to a high interest rate.

The worst deals come from 'weekly collected credit' where door-to-door moneylenders offer cash loans in return for high weekly repayments, typically over 10 to 50 weeks. Here interest rates can legally hit 200 per cent or even 1,000 per cent. These loans are aimed at those who cannot get credit easily – or who don't know better.

Watch out too for shopping catalogues which offer 'free' credit. These are brought to your home by local 'agents' who receive a 10 per cent commission on your purchases. While the interest rate is zero, catalogue companies make up for this by charging far more for the goods than a high street shop. A 'Christmas hamper' purchased in this way can cost nearly twice as much as the same items in a supermarket.

Buy a major item such as a new kitchen, new windows, a car or a caravan and the salesperson tends to be more concerned with how you will pay for the item than with stressing its intrinsic value. This is not because they are worried about your ability to pay but so they can try to sell high commission loans. The salesperson may receive more for your signature on a loan agreement than for selling the goods themselves.

Instead, for £1,000 to £15,000 of credit that can be repaid over one to five years, try a bank, supermarket bank or building society for a personal loan. These set a fixed rate of interest for the loan term so you can budget the cost. You will not benefit if interest rates fall (though you will gain if they rise). Some will charge a penalty of around two to three months' interest if you repay the loan ahead of schedule. Paying back over a longer period produces lower monthly instalments but a higher overall cost. The larger the amount you borrow, the lower the rate should be. But shop around – there is a big gap between best and worst, especially if you have a good credit rating. You do not have to take the loan your own bank or building society sells.

Many loans come in two versions – with or without insurance. This cover pays the loan instalments when you are out of work due to sickness, accident or redundancy. The premiums are high in relation to the potential payout. Some plans only protect you for a number of months, and you may have to be out of work for two months or longer before you can claim. The rules are tough – you will not be paid if your redundancy is voluntary, if you are self-employed or on short-term contracts or if you conceivably knew about the chance of losing your job when you signed up. Costs can be as high as £20 extra a month on a £150 monthly repayment. A minority need this cover and few ever qualify for a claim. But banks earn substantial sums for selling these plans.

Personal loans are 'unsecured'. Like credit card debts and store credits borrowings, lenders cannot take your home away if you default. They must go to court firstly to force you to pay, although ultimately they can file for your personal bankruptcy or send in bailiffs.

Your home is at risk if you take out a secured loan such as a 'second mortgage'. These loans can be identified from adverts saying 'no tenants' or 'homeowners only'. With these, you continue to pay your original mortgage. But if you default on your second loan, the lender can attempt to repossess the property no matter how far advanced you are with the first mortgage. Interest rates can be very high – and there are often tough penalties for repaying the loan early.

A 'remortgage' is altogether different. Here you repay your first mortgage completely and start again with a new loan, usually on better interest rate terms than the first. A remortgage can also enable homeowners to release some of the value of their property into cash. Someone who bought a house for £50,000 with a £40,000 loan ten years ago might find it is now worth £100,000 with £35,000 still outstanding. They remortgage for 70 per cent of the property's value and receive £70,000. They use £35,000 to pay off the original home loan leaving £35,000 for other uses. The amount they can borrow is limited by the earnings of the homebuyer and partner and the maximum percentage of the value of the home the loan company is offering.

The interest rate on mortgages will generally be lower than on any other form of borrowing, outside of promotional deals. But you could end up breaking one of the 'rules' of borrowing. Provided you are young enough, you could arrange the new loan over as long as 25 years. But that is an expensive way of repaying an amount borrowed for an asset such as a car that will have to be replaced far sooner. You can, however, arrange for part of the remortgage to be repaid more rapidly than the rest.

Debt difficulties

Some people get into debt difficulties because they are spendaholics. They apply for every credit facility on offer, push it to the limit and then beyond. It is not difficult for those with a good credit record to arrange £25,000 or even £50,000 worth of borrowing during just one day in a city centre shopping area.

However, most debt problems occur because of external events – job loss, death or serious illness, or a relationship breakdown. Once the demands start to come in red, it is time to take action. Trying to ignore the problem or burning the bills will not help, it will make matters worse.

If the situation has not gone too far, you may be able to retrieve it yourself by cutting down on expenses and trying to increase your income by taking on extra paid work. Other possibilities include taking in a lodger and checking to see if you qualify for any state benefits. Drawing up a budget showing your spending will help trim your outgoings. But if that is not enough, you will need outside help. Some local authorities have free debt advice centres. A local Citizens Advice Bureau office will either direct you to one or, possibly, arrange for one of its own experts to see you. National Debtline (0808 8084000) offers advice over the phone.

Take care before agreeing to a 'loan consolidation' package. This is where a new lender offers a loan large enough to pay off all your other borrowings on the theory that one big loan will be cheaper to pay off – as well as offering a fresh start. Often, the new loan will have lower monthly payments but you will have to pay it off over a very long period. It might also be secured, so your home is now at risk. Loan consolidation can be out of the frying pan and into the fire. Here are some debt dos and don'ts:

- Don't ignore the problem – it will not go away.
- Work out your income and essential expenditure.
- Check on potential benefits and tax rebates.
- Talk to your creditors – if you tell them you have difficulties they might be more sympathetic. They would rather be paid over a longer period than have the hassle of going to court and ending up with very little.
- Don't borrow from Peter to pay Paul – taking out more credit just means more trouble.
- Arrange your debts in order of priority – not in order of the debtor who shouts loudest or who threatens most. Bills connected with your home such as the mortgage or rent, water, gas and electricity are the most vital. Council tax, income tax and national insurance (where applicable) come next. Credit cards, catalogues and other consumer loans have less immediate importance.
- Avoid fee charging 'debt management' companies.
- Make offers to creditors.
- Cut up all credit and store cards.

If you are threatened with repossession of your home or disconnection of a power supply, seek help at once. Never make yourself voluntarily homeless by moving out and posting the keys of your home to your mortgage lender.

2
Health and Wealth

Looking after it

No matter how hard you work, how frantically you save, and how brilliantly you arrange your finances, all this effort and planning can be undone if you fall seriously ill or die prematurely. This grim possibility leaves you with four choices:

- Hope it does not happen – in the great majority of cases, it will not happen. Most people get through their working and earning lives with little interruption from serious illness. And most people live long enough to collect their pensions – life expectancy increased by around 20 years during the twentieth century and illnesses declined dramatically. We are healthier and longer-living than ever before.
- Rely on state benefits if you cannot work. These are not generous but are just about sufficient to hold body and soul together. You pay for these benefits through taxation whether you want them or not – so you might as well claim them wherever possible. They also represent a backstop for those who take the 'hope it never happens' course – no matter how misplaced your optimism, there is a social security safety net.
- Spend your savings to tide you over difficult periods. This depends, of course, on having these in the first place.
- Insure against possible eventualities. This is costly – the more so as you reach an age where death is more common or if insurers believe you have a lifestyle that represents a higher than average chance of death or sickness – you may have to pay more if you are a gay man,

or if you have an occupation that insurers consider a threat to life and limb such as being a test pilot or a steeplejack.

If you decide on the insurance route, you will have to work out just what you want, and – more importantly – how much you can afford. Don't expect too much guidance from the insurance industry. It wants to sell policies and the bigger, the better. Its costs in selling a £10,000 plan are little different from selling one for £1 million.

Various companies suggest insuring your life for anything from three times your annual earnings to as much as twenty times. But such surveys – which always seem to produce results that are favourable to their marketing line – always say we do not have enough insurance. Their target, of course, always moves ahead of what people actually buy. So ignore their so-called research and, within the limits of affordability, look at what your real needs might be and how much you might have from other sources.

Protection insurance falls into two main categories – policies that pay out on death and those that pay should you contract certain medical conditions or be incapacitated by accident. Anyone can insure their lives for almost any value whatsoever – there is no such thing as 'over-insurance', only what you can afford.

Life insurance – cover against death – is only worth having if there is someone who relies on you for money and would therefore face financial problems from your demise. If you are single, in a relationship where your partner does not depend on you, or married without children where your spouse earns enough to be independent, you may find that life insurance is not necessary. Insurance sellers say you should have at least enough cover to pay off mortgages and other loans. But again, if there is no one to pick up the property on your demise, all you are doing is covering the bank or loan company.

Equally, there is often little point in insuring your life once you reach an age where death starts to stare you in the face. The older you are, the more expensive cover is. Insurance companies are not charities – they work out the odds of having to pay so they are unlikely to offer any great bargains to those in their seventies or older. That said, there could be reasons why you might buy life insurance at these ages where your dependants face paying inheritance tax.

Before even considering life cover, look to check whether you have some already. You may have some insurance through your work, especially if you are employed by a major organisation. And you may have acquired some cover through old policies and friendly society plans.

Life insurance: how it works

There are two main types of life insurance policy – those that cover your life for a fixed period and plans that can last throughout your life. The first is known as term insurance, the second whole-of-life. Both can be combined with an investment policy that has a value irrespective of whether there is a death claim. Bundling the two elements into an 'endowment policy' together is now controversial. It makes it far harder to see what is going on and whether each part represents good value. Persuading a customer to buy an endowment produces far greater commission for the seller than a straight protection policy. Protect yourself by always insisting that the seller justifies the endowment recommendation in writing – and check the advice is fair by consulting others.

Term assurance is the most basic type of life cover. It simply agrees to pay a fixed sum if you die during the period the policy lasts, providing you have kept up the monthly payments. But nothing is ever that simple.

The first variable is the term itself – how long do you want the cover to last? Mainstream policies generally run from ten to 25 or 30 years, although specialist insurers will offer cover for shorter periods – sometimes as little as a few days if the policy buyer has special, usually work-related, reasons. Assuming you know why you want the cover, then it should be easier to work out the term. For many, this might be the number of years before children are off your hands; for others, it could

Save £'s on your life insurance.

life direct

We independently search the entire market for the best premium for your circumstances, then apply a discount to take it down even further.

Click www.lifedirect.com
or ring 0800 970 0457 for a FREE quotation.

Save money. Cut the cost of your life insurance – instantly!

If you have taken out a life insurance policy in the last five years, or are considering one now, LifeSearch will save you money. We compare hundreds of quotes from leading companies to get you the same cover for <u>considerably</u> less.

£100,000 of Life Cover

Abbey National Life	£39.64
Nationwide Life	£20.70
Virgin	£16.26
M & S	£15.25
Eagle Star Direct	£14.66
LifeSearch	**£11.20**

Call LifeSearch direct on

0800 316 3166

Anytime 8.00am to 8.00pm weekdays and weekends

Please quote reference FFL 1

www.lifesearch.co.uk

*Life*SEARCH

We search. You save.

Premiums based on a monthly cost, with a leading insurer, for 25 year level term life cover for a non-smoking man aged 35 next birthday in normal health. Figures correct at 01.05.01

be the period before the mortgage is paid off; and for a third group, it might be up to retirement.

The monthly premiums on a ten-year plan are lower than on a longer-term policy. But if your needs are to cover the next 20 years, then it makes sense to buy a 20 year plan now. Turning it into two ten year terms is likely to be more expensive – and you may suffer a lifestyle or health change over the first ten years which will make the second period prohibitively expensive or even impossible to obtain. Once you have signed up to a plan, the insurer has to honour it even if your health deteriorates or if you no longer fit the lifestyle requirements.

You can, however, walk away from a term assurance plan at any time by cancelling the premiums. Term plans have no cash-in value (other than on death) so you will have received nothing other than the peace of mind that your dependants are protected. This is also true if you stick with the policy for the whole term.

You can cover yourself or buy a joint policy that also pays out if your partner dies. Most of these work on the basis that the sum insured is paid on the first death. Buying a joint policy is more expensive than for one person – the risk of a death is greater – but far cheaper than taking out two separate policies as the insurance company only has one payment to contemplate.

There are a number of factors insurance companies take into account when setting term and other life insurance premiums.

1. *Your age now* (or that of a partner as well if you have a joint policy). The younger you are, the lower the premiums.
2. *Your sex.* Women live longer on average than men so insurers set lower premiums for females. Young men, in particular, are seen by some companies as a poor proposition due to the relatively high number of accidental and violent deaths suffered by this age group.
3. *Your sexuality.* Insurers do not like gay men – they panicked when AIDs/HIV first appeared in the 1980s and while some have calmed down since, expect to find discrimination. Some insist on HIV tests – and then proceed to load the premiums because you have taken a

test. There are a number of specialist brokers who look for better deals for homosexual men.

4. *Your occupation.* If insurers think there is a physical or lifestyle risk associated with your job, they may increase premiums.

5. *Whether you smoke.* Virtually all companies now have two premium scales – one for those who smoke and lower rates for those who do not. Insurers believe that the likelihood of death is higher for smokers at any age – some say that smokers are more likely to have other habits they disapprove of even if there is no firm evidence of this. Insurers do not need to justify their ratings to anyone other than their own shareholders. To qualify for non-smoker rates, you must either never have smoked or have given up at least 12 to 24 months ago (the period depends on the company). If you take up smoking again, you should inform the insurance company. Otherwise, it could refuse to pay out should you die or pay out a smaller sum as you have broken the terms of the contract. In practice, insurers rarely quibble. They realise that the need for an autopsy, plus a possible row with remaining family and the fact that the one person who really knows is now dead all add up to a potential public relations disaster which could cost more than paying up. Many, but not all, non-smoking policies allow for the occasional, celebratory cigar.

6. *Your present and past health record.* All life company proposal forms ask you about your health. Insurers want to know if there is anything past or present that increases your risk of dying. If you have had a medical problem in the past – even if you have now fully recovered – you should reveal this. Insurers can tear up policies on the grounds of 'non-disclosure', although refusing to pay a death claim is rare unless fraud is suspected – there have been cases of non-existent lives being insured.

If you want to insure your life for a very large sum (from £250,000 to £500,000 and upwards) the insurer can insist on you taking a medical examination carried out by a doctor of its choice. For somewhat lower sums – the figures vary substantially between companies – insurers will ask your own doctor for a report on your health. Companies must ask your permission for this, although anyone withholding this is unlikely to get much further in the process. You are legally entitled to see a copy of any medical report.

Insurers say 95 per cent of people who fill in proposal forms are accepted at normal rates and without any conditions being imposed. But this does not mean that 95 per cent of the population are healthy enough to impress the insurers. Many of those who might not qualify do not bother to apply in the first place. If an insurer turns you down or insists on special premiums or other conditions, you are required to reveal this on any subsequent proposals. Obviously, other insurers are hardly likely to accept someone with open arms who has been rejected elsewhere.

If you fear being turned down on the grounds of present or past health problems, find a broker who specialises in 'impaired lives' policies rather than risk rejection when applying for yourself. Experts in this field know which insurers are likely to prove sympathetic to someone with your type of medical history and may be able to find one who will insure at normal rates. Failing that they could recommend:

- paying extra –four times or more in some cases;
- restricting the policy so that it only pays out for death due to conditions other than those you already have;
- reducing payouts if you die within a fixed period – the rest of the policy could revert to normal if your health improves.

It is nearly always possible to get insurance at a price – some insurance brokers set up death-bed policies as part of complicated tax saving strategies. It can also be worth contacting charities that specialise in your medical complaint – they often have contacts that can result in a better insurance deal.

Term assurance policies should be 'written in trust' to avoid future inheritance tax charges (see Chapter 7).

Term cover options

Most term policies have a fixed premium with a fixed payout for a fixed time period. If you are still alive at the end – most people are – the policy is worthless and can be torn up. Insurers call these basic policies 'level term'. But there are variations – most of which increase the premiums.

- Renewable term policies allow holders to buy a second plan on the expiry of the first without further medical questioning or examinations.
- Convertible term plans mean the holder can 'upgrade' to whole-of-life or endowment plans without further medicals.
- Decreasing term is used in conjunction with mortgages and other loans – as the loan repayments are made to cut the amount owed, the cover required and therefore payout amount goes down as well. Towards the end of the term, the potential payout could be small.
- Increasing term – both cover and premiums go up each year either in line with inflation or a set percentage.
- Family Income Benefit – a little used concept that can save money. Instead of paying a lump sum on death, these plans offer a fixed monthly sum for the remainder of the policy term – if the holder dies exactly three years before the end of the plan, there will be 36 monthly payments.

Whole-of-life insurance

These plans were heavily sold during the 1970s and 1980s by commission-chasing insurance salespeople. Students and other young people were prime targets. But since these policies only pay out on death and became valueless once a month's contribution was missed, many owners faced a long haul – possibly 60 years although some insurers say premiums can stop when the holder reaches 85. Unsurprisingly, many of the policies have been left to expire worthless.

Some are pure protection with fixed premiums and fixed payments – which could have little value as even 2 per cent annual inflation would halve the real worth of a plan in 35 years. Others have a built-in investment element and regular increases in premiums – usually at five-year intervals.

Are they worth it? If you don't have one, it is hard to find a lifestyle that requires non-stop protection at a relatively high price. The one exception to this can be in some tax saving strategies, but these only apply to an elderly, well-off audience.

If you have one, see if it fits in with your protection needs. Ask yourself, does it have any point? It may never have done so other than providing an income for an insurance seller. Could you buy more suitable and greater cover from term insurance for the same money or less? Is there a surrender value? It will not be great but could possibly be useful. Could you use the premiums more sensibly on other savings or spending? Do you really want to continue paying until the day you die or you reach a very advanced age?

Before ditching a policy, always check that you can set up a replacement plan if you need to. If your health has severely deteriorated, you may find you cannot buy a new scheme.

Replacing income

What happens if you fall ill and can no longer earn a living? The state benefit scheme does offer some help but much is means-tested, so ruling out anyone with more than a modicum of savings. Life insurance is no use here – you have to be dead to claim. But the insurance industry has a wide range of policies designed to offer a lump sum in cash or a regular income in the event of serious or long lasting illness. These policies are not cheap – the chances of calling on this form of cover are higher than those of dying. Nor is there the competitive pressure that is currently forcing term rates lower.

Protection purchasers have two main routes to consider – income replacement plans (most are technically known as Permanent Health

Insurance or PHI) and critical illness policies. Critical illness plans, which pay out a lump sum when one of a number of serious medical conditions is diagnosed, will be examined later in this section.

Government figures show that at any one time, nearly two million people below retirement age will have been off work for at least six months due to sickness or disability. Many of these are on long term government benefits. The basic non-means-tested statutory sick pay is just over £62 a week. But more importantly, there is nothing extra for partners or children whether dependent or not. Means-tested payments are more generous but a working partner – whether married or not – or more than minimal savings will usually rule these out.

You may have a workplace illness and disability scheme. Some can be generous; others less so; and many are non-existent – especially if you work for a small firm. In any case, the self-employed or those in casual or short-term contract work will not be covered.

Whichever you look at, the basic rule of insurance pricing applies – the more you are likely to claim, the more you have to pay. Income replacement plans are the more expensive of the two. Most are geared to the needs of employees – and the great majority of these are sold to firms who want to cover their staff. But you can also buy plans as an individual employee, as a self-employed person, – even for a non-working spouse.

The theory of the housewife/househusband style of cover is that replacing the domestic work that an ill or disabled partner would have carried out is expensive – this much for chauffeuring, childcare, cookery, domestic appliance maintenance, DIY and so on. But while totting up the value of a non-working spouse can make for amusing magazine articles – £20,000 a year is one recent guess – the reality is that very few of these policies are sold. Moreover, most houseperson policies have a much lower maximum level of cover.

There are two main income protection routes – limited term and long term. The first costs less but only provides an income for up to one or two years. The second is designed to pay out a regular sum until the day you would have retired, if necessary. Short term income replacement is of relatively little value – if you are going to be unable to work for the rest of your life, one or two years' worth of monthly income is a help but not much more. Many can cope with the first months of not earning thanks to savings.

Unlike life insurance, an income replacement policy is worth considering if you are single and have no dependents – after all, you have to have an income as long as you live. But if you are in a stable relationship and your partner has a good enough income on which both of you could live, then it could be hard to justify the expense – and PHI is expensive. It is costly because less serious illnesses can prevent you working for months or possibly forever. These need not be life threatening; arthritis in the hand or fingers could end employment requiring keyboard skills; and back conditions could stop work requiring physical activity.

PHI income protection plans pay an agreed percentage of your current earnings – usually between 50 and 65 per cent, although some companies have schemes to pay to 75 per cent of your wage packet – obviously the higher the ratio, the more expensive the premiums.

Most PHI policies are tailor-made to suit individual circumstances, and you have substantial control over the cost by mixing and matching factors affecting premium level. These include:

- *Your age* – the younger you are when you start, the less you pay. But it is not quite as simple as with life insurance because an insurer would have to pay out more for a younger person who cannot work over the years.
- *Your sex* – there are no laws to prevent discrimination and in PHI, this is applied with a vengeance. In most plans, women pay a third to a half more than men. Insurers say women are far more likely to claim but they admit that this is based on the very small number of women who have bought plans.
- *Your sexual orientation* – the usual prejudice against gay men applies in most plans.

- *The selected retirement age* – PHI pays until the chosen age so the younger this is, the lower the premiums. Opting for 65 instead of 60 can double the cost of some plans – the longer the policy lasts the more the chance of claiming and payments will have to go on for longer.

- *The 'deferment' or waiting period* – PHI plans are not geared to pay out from the first day of sickness. So you cannot claim every time you have a day off for a cold. Instead, there is a waiting period, which can range from anything from one month to two years. This gives the flexibility to fit in with either savings or a company scheme, which has a limited life. The longer the deferment period, the lower the premiums will be.

- *The level of replacement earnings required* – obviously higher percentages require higher premiums. But you can also build in annual inflation or other upgrades – again this is more expensive.

- *Your present occupation* – insurers have up to five levels of risk. Work that involves physical danger such as the army or police is virtually uninsurable but in this case the employer – the government – provides cover. Also, it is not just traditional manual work that attracts high premiums – professional musicians who can be out of work after suffering minor finger injuries are higher rated. Office workers tend to have the lowest premium rating.

- *What occupation do you have to be unable to do before you can claim?* The most expensive definition is 'own occupation' – this will pay out if you can no longer do your own normal work. So if your job involves driving and you can no longer control a car, you can have a claim. 'Any suitable occupation' is wider – here the idea is you can claim if you cannot do your own job or any other fitted to your personality and qualifications. 'Any occupation' means you have to be unable to do any work – even jobs that are far from your normal line in both money and qualifications – before you can claim. Since this is least likely it is the cheapest cover option. Some insurers now use a 'works task' definition instead of 'any occupation', where you can claim if you are unable to do a number of everyday job tasks such as reading, lifting, walking and talking on the phone.

Critical illness insurance

Twenty years ago, insurance company executives noticed that they were paying out on fewer life insurance policies. People were living longer, and the number of policyholders who died was substantially reduced. In the short term, this meant a profit – they would pay out fewer claims while continuing to take in premiums. But over the longer term, they realised that life insurance rates would plummet. They were right.

However, they also noticed that while fewer people in a given age group died, just as many continued to contract serious medical problems such as heart attacks or cancer, which effectively ended their working lives. They also noticed that those contracting these critical health problems lived far longer than previously after the diagnosis thanks to modern medical methods such as new drugs or surgical intervention. But the families of victims could neither claim on a life policy as the policyholder was still alive nor enjoy a reasonable standard of living as the policyholder was no longer earning.

So 'dread disease' policies were invented, which paid out on the diagnosis of a number of medical conditions providing that the policyholder lived more than a set number of days – usually 30. Dread disease was renamed critical illness and is now offered by virtually every life insurance company.

It is more expensive than 'plain vanilla' life cover as you are more likely to contract a serious illness within a given time period than to die.

Almost every insurer uses the same statistics in presentations to prospective policy purchasers to show this – and how long you could live after contracting the illness. These figures come from charities covering various medical conditions.

- An estimated 180,000 a year develop dementia associated with old age such as Alzheimer's Disease.
- One million people a year are diagnosed with head injuries – 45 per cent of those with severe head injuries will not work again.
- One in three will have cancer diagnosed at some point in their life – but more than half will survive for at least five years.

- There are 330,000 heart attacks a year but two thirds of males will survive at least five years.
- Nearly 20,000 people are receiving kidney dialysis.
- There are 85,000 with multiple sclerosis.
- There are 120,000 with Parkinson's disease.
- Around 100,000 suffer their first stroke each year.
- One in four men and one in five women will contract a serious illness before they reach 65.

If these statistics frighten, they are meant to. But they do need to be seen in context. For example, while one million might have head injuries a year, relatively few are serious so the 45 per cent is of a substantially lower figure than one million. And the vast majority of the above illnesses and conditions occur in those approaching or past retirement age. For someone aged 25, asked by an adviser to buy this insurance to cover a 25-year mortgage, the chances are far smaller than these statistics imply. But if you do consider this form of policy worthwhile, it is both a competitive market and one where there are several ways of purchasing the cover.

Most policies are term – they give cover for a set period. But you can buy the more expensive whole-of-life version, which will pay out at any time in your life providing you continue with the premiums. You can buy the cover on a 'standalone' basis so it would only pay out if you contracted a disease on the list and survived for a set period. Or you can opt for 'first event' where the policy pays out on disease diagnosis or on death, whichever occurs first during the duration of the policy. This is more costly than standalone as the risks are greater. Or you can have a still more expensive policy that pays out both on diagnosis and on death – but this would only pay out once if death were due to a condition not covered by the policy or through an accident. Policies can cover individuals as well as couples who are married or in heterosexual partnerships.

Underwriting – the costing of the risk by the insurance company – is similar to that involved in life cover. Companies look at age, sex, medical history, occupation, whether you smoke, as well as the length of the policy. You can insure for any sum you wish – providing you can afford the premiums. The average policy is for around £50,000. Many policies give the option to increase the cover for additional payments on certain occasions such as a new child or moving home and taking out a larger mortgage.

Traditional life insurance needs little explanation. If the policyholder dies, there should be a payout. Few policies now apply a suicide exclusion. Critical illness is different. Not all policies cover the same conditions; and even if they do, their definition of when an illness becomes a claim can differ. But most policies now adhere to the Association of British Insurers' 'model wordings'. These set a minimum standard for critical illness. All policies should include:

- cancer;
- coronary artery by-pass surgery;
- heart attack;
- kidney failure;
- major organ (including bone marrow) transplant;
- multiple sclerosis;
- stroke.

Additional conditions covered by most policies include:

- aorta graft surgery;
- benign brain tumour;
- blindness;
- coma;
- deafness;
- heart valve replacement or repair;
- loss of limbs;
- loss of speech;
- motor neurone disease (usually before a set age);
- paralysis/paraplegia;
- Parkinson's disease (usually before a set age);
- terminal illness (where you are diagnosed with less than a year to live);
- third degree burns.

However, some medical conditions are specifically excluded from policies:

- AIDS/HIV;
- those resulting from aviation other than in commercial aircraft;
- those resulting from criminal acts – other than being a victim;
- those resulting from drug and other substance abuse;
- those resulting from failure to follow medical advice;
- those resulting from hazardous sports and pastimes including boxing, martial arts, mountaineering and yacht-racing;
- those occurring when you are living abroad – outside the European Union for more than 13 consecutive weeks in any one year;
- self-inflicted injury;
- skin cancers;
- those resulting from war and civil commotion.

Should you buy critical illness or life insurance if your budget is limited? Look at factors such as:

- Do you have dependants? If not, then critical illness cover is more important as you could use the money to help adapt your home or pay for living expenses.
- Do you already have life cover either from a private policy or with your work? Then opt for critical illness policies so you are not duplicating your insurance.
- Have you got a good income replacement policy? Then go for life cover although you will miss out on the lump sum that critical illness can provide.

Needless to say, insurance sellers try to persuade you to buy every form of insurance in this section. That would give 'peace of mind' but there is no point signing up for policies where you are unable to continue paying premiums.

PERSONAL TOUCH FINANCE

If you have not already heard about us, Personal Touch Finance is a well-established, originally family run, company based in the West Midlands. We now offer a full and comprehensive range of independent financial advice through a nationwide network of advisers. Our Head Office has 70 experienced staff that are consistently trained and updated on the changes taking place in the market place. We are based at Cheshire House, High Street, Knowle, West Midlands B93 0LL.

As a Company, we are dedicated to providing an outstanding quality of service. We are not perfect, but we strive to be the best. We recognise that customers are at the heart of our business and therefore take pride in providing a service built on a relationship of innovation, trust and partnership.

Our many professional advisers will be happy to provide you with confidential advice for both your own personal financial needs as well as those of your company.

- Competitively priced Life Insurance
- Up to date information on a wide range of investments and the companies that provide them
- Technical advice on Trust and Inheritance Tax Planning
- We can help you with Retirement Planning (including stakeholder pensions)
- We can source the best mortgage on the marketplace for you*
- We can offer you a totally independent general insurance service for buildings, contents, car, etc.*

* These products are not regulated by the Personal Investment Authority

This comprehensive service has grown out of the large investment we have made in acquiring advanced technology, including a computerised back office administration system and 'state of the art' software packages to source the best deals around. We are continually developing new products and creating market leaders. By contacting us, we can assure you that you will have access to all the best packages available at the touch of a button backed up by that 'personal touch' of friendly and helpful staff.

For more information you can visit our website.
www.theinsurancesupermarket.com

Alternatively, please telephone us on
01564 206250
and ask for Richard.

Personal Touch Finance is a trading style of
Personal Touch Insurance Services Ltd
which is regulated by the
Personal Investment Authority

Invest through Torquil Clark and get on the fast track to more informed investment decisions

Informed investors are more successful investors and you'll find thousands of them at Torquil Clark. Just visit our website and you'll see why. Our clients have exclusive access to our Members Lounge, where they can track the performance of their investments, catch up on the latest money news and learn of new investment opportunities. You'll also find investment fund spotlights and direct online dealing facilities, at very low cost indeed. We shelter our clients from unwanted junk mail, hold twice yearly investment seminars, and keep them briefed by our popular bulletins. So for ISAs, ISA Transfers, PEP Transfers, Unit Trusts and Pensions – talk to Torquil Clark.

0800 413186

www.tqonline.co.uk

TORQUIL CLARK plc
The value brokers

3
Making It Work for You

Anyone with spare money should make it work as hard as possible. But they have to weigh up potential returns against the risks involved – and what they want from their savings.

Those in the fortunate position of having money to spare can be savers, investors, or both – they can save part of their cash and invest the rest. Here saving generally means with a bank, building society or similar organisation. You should earn some interest on your money but the original cash should be safe. By contrast investment normally involves risk – the return could be higher than savings but equally you could end up with less than you started with. All investments work on the basis of the higher the hoped for return, the higher the risk. No one will pay more than the going savings rate unless there is a chance you might have to give them some of your money. This chapter looks first at saving then at investments.

Saving it

You will almost certainly have some savings at some time – a smaller proportion buy investments.

You are a saver if:

- you have a goal for your money. This could be a major expenditure on a car, a caravan, a holiday home, home improvements, or perhaps a dream holiday or a child's wedding. You may not know exactly when you will need to pay for these but you are sure you will at some stage – and that you do not want to go into debt to pay for them.

- you put by an emergency fund – 'rainy day' money – that will pay for repairing the roof, sorting out the car, buying air tickets to visit family abroad if someone becomes seriously ill, and any of hundreds of other contingencies.
- you are trying to put together a deposit on a home.
- you want to open your own business and fund the start-up and stocking costs without having to go begging to a bank manager.
- you have educational costs – either school fees or university expenses.
- you have high earnings now but worry about the future when it could all dry up.
- you are retired and cannot afford to take any risks with your money.

Most of these are long term projects that would fail to materialise if you invested unwisely, although there is nothing to stop anyone taking risks if they have sufficient money elsewhere to meet these costs. Most people also save short-term – they are paid once a month and have to make the money last as long as possible.

Risk-free saving involves banks, building societies, some insurance companies, and the government-backed National Savings. The object is to earn as much as possible in interest while retaining the access to your cash that you require.

There are some basic rules:

- The more accessible your money, the lower the interest rate tends to be. If you want 24 hour a day access to your savings via a cash machine, the ability to write cheques, or easy access to a bank or building society branch, expect lower returns, often as low as a tiny fraction of one per cent.
- Tying up your money for a period is the only way of guaranteeing a known interest rate. Most interest rates are variable – great if they are rising but miserable if they fall. Some savings institutions offer fixed rate accounts. But you have to agree to tie your money up for a set period.

Pick up
rock solid returns

Gartmore Stable Growth Fund

Introducing an exciting new Fund from one of the UK's leading fund management houses.

- **Investing in low risk Zero Dividend Preference Shares**
- **Aims to provide steady capital growth**
- **Take capital growth as a form of tax free** income**
- **Helps you plan for your future**

Utilising your capital gains tax allowance the anticipated returns are **7%** gross p.a.* This would equate to an impressive **11.6%** p.a. pre-tax interest from a deposit account for higher rate tax payers.

The level of yield can fluctuate and is not guaranteed.
Your money is more secure in a deposit account.

Pick up a brochure, call 0800 289 336

*Expect*more, *Get*more,

Gartmore

www.gartmore.com

CHELSEA FINANCIAL SERVICES
MD DARIUS MCDERMOTT
OFFERS SOME FINANCIAL ADVICE

When investing a lump sum, whether for income or growth, the main consideration will be the return you wish to achieve. The underlying charges payable in the investment play a crucial part of this. There is a wide range of choice for a lump sum investment and there are many factors to consider when making that choice. Attitude to risk, your tax position, a need for income or capital growth, perhaps an ethical approach, or the length of time that you wish to hold an investment.

Chelsea Financial Services offers discounts on a variety of bespoke products, including Unit Trusts and OEICs; ISAs; Investment Bonds; and Venture Capital Trusts. We also offer significant discounts on PEP and ISA transfers. The original investment choice will rarely remain suitable for the very long term. We also provide a PEP and ISA Appraisal Service, at no extra cost, to enable our clients to consider adjustments when they are required.

The amount of tax payable within or on encashment of an investment is important too. ISAs appear at the top of the selection list here because of their tax status. An ISA is a tax wrapper for a variety of investments including cash, insurance, shares and unit trusts.

The maximum investment is restricted to £7,000 because it is tax free. There is a massive choice of funds available for this. Chelsea Financial Services offer discounts of up to 5.25% on lump sums invested in funds with companies such as ABN AMRO, Aberdeen, Jupiter and New Star. This means a saving of £367.85 on a £7,000 investment.

Investors often save the maximum allowed in this way to build up a tax free portfolio of unit trusts, OEICs, investment trusts and shares. This has many uses. It may the method of saving used to repay a mortgage. The tax status enhances the growth within the plan, there is no tax on encashment and the ability to encash ISAs at any time without penalty means that the mortgage loan may be reduced earlier than planned, if they have achieved an impressive performance.

This means that the interest payments for the mortgage loan can be reduced. If your ISA portfolio is achieving a higher return than the interest rate you are paying on your mortgage, then it is not logical to repay the loan early.

A portfolio of ISA investments is often used to supplement income in retirement. Pensions are relatively restricted. Of course, there is tax relief given on every premium paid and a portion of the plan paid out as a tax free lump sum. However, the earliest age for taking out a pension income is 50 and the government are looking to raise this. You have no access to the major portion of the fund saved, which must used to purchase an annuity which produces the pension income. ISAs are flexible. They may be set up initially for growth then for income – all tax free. The risk profile can be altered at will. The capital is accessible at any time, regardless of age or the term of the investment. The discounts given by Chelsea Financial Services ensure that any changes made to the ISA portfolio are made at a low cost, maintaining the value of the investments.

If you have used up your £7,000 ISA allowance, then you can invest in plain Unit Trusts or Open Ended Investment Companies (OEICs). Providers include such companies as SocGen, INVESCO Perpetual and Merrill Lynch. On a lump sum investment of £50,000+, even bigger discounts can be negotiated.

Investment Bonds are attractive because of their tax treatment. The basic rate tax payer has no further tax liability as this is payable within the bond itself. Higher rate taxpayers can defer encashment of the bond until they no longer have the higher rate tax liability. Also, 5% income can be withdrawn from the bond tax free. Chelsea Financial Services will typically discount these investments by 2%. If the investment is £100,000+ then this is negotiable up to 5.5%, a saving of £5,500.

Investment Bonds are useful for Inheritance Tax Planning, where 101% of the value of the fund is paid to the estate on death. The plan can be written in trusts, when the value of the plan is paid directly to the named beneficiary. This way the value of the estate can be geared to stay below the Inheritance Tax threshold which is currently £242,000. There are different types of trust available and sometimes legal advice is appropriate.

Venture Capital Trusts (VCTs), as their name suggests, are not for the cautious investor. They are popular for deferring Capital Gains Tax and for their other tax breaks. The shares must be held for three years to qualify for the initial 20% income tax relief. Chelsea Financial Services will refund 50% of the commission received on these lump sum investments, for example, the Unicorn AIM VCT. Many people assume that the cheapest route for investment is to go direct to the investment company, cutting out the middle man. Wrong in my opinion. Going direct often means you pay the full charges which the provider hangs on to – Chelsea Financial Services is happy to rebate those charges, working on the principle that it is better to earn a little from a lot of people.

For more details, call 020 7384 7300 or visit www.chelseafs.co.uk

- The top rates are away from the high street. Most of the 'best buy' savings deals come from phone or post or internet-based bank and building society accounts.

- You have to be nifty to get the best rates. Accounts are set up with attractive rates but often slip back to the average, to mediocrity or to downright rip-off levels. So you have to be ready to move your money to chase the top deals.

- If you are prepared to give notice before withdrawing money (notice accounts), you should get a little more.

- Larger amounts tend to attract better interest rates – it can be worth-while for a savings company to pay 0.5 per cent more if you keep £5,000 rather than £500 in an account.

- Lesser known banks and building societies often pay more. But always check that your savings are covered by a compensation scheme if there is a problem. Banks and building societies can go bust. There is a UK compensation scheme covering the first £20,000; offshore accounts may have no such safety net.

- Not all accounts are what they seem. Some 'instant access' accounts offer high rates but only allow instant access on two or three occasions a year. Otherwise, savers have to pay a penalty. Interest rates might be boosted by 'bonuses', which are withdrawn after a period.

- Banks and building societies that offer 'notice' accounts usually allow immediate access to cash if the accountholder foregoes the same amount of interest – on a 90 day notice account, you should get to your money immediately by paying a 90 day interest rate penalty. But some want both.

With well over 100 savings organisations and more than 1,000 accounts, savers can find exceptions to all these rules. But it is always worth asking why an account with certain features is so much better – or worse – than similar offerings from rivals. It might often be due to hidden, small print details.

There is little independent advice on savings accounts. Only a tiny handful of banks – usually connected to life insurance companies – pay advisers anything for recommending their products so most savers will be on their own and have to do their own research.

Newspapers and magazines print 'best buy' tables, covering a whole range of bank related financial areas such as mortgages, personal loans, current accounts, savings accounts, home and motor insurance. Many also feature past performance figures from endowments, unit trusts and investment trusts. These can be very useful if you have the time and inclination to be able to switch your money around at short notice.

The Internet makes this easier but not nearly as easy as it is to carry out other financial transactions such as buying and selling shares or purchasing holiday insurance. One reason is that every bank and building society is paranoid about 'money laundering'. This is where criminals take tainted cash and try to turn it into respectable money. To prevent this, financial companies insist on identity checks when you open an account. This can be tiresome, especially to older people who may not have a driving licence or passport or workplace identification. So once you have opened an account, think twice before closing it completely. It can be worth leaving behind a nominal £1 – £100 in a mutual building society just in case it decides to demutualise and hand over windfalls to members. That way, you can always revive a relationship with a bank or building society without too much bureaucracy.

However, if you are eager to spend your leisure time shifting money around, be aware of the dangers of best buy tables. While every publication offers the tables as a reader service with the best of intentions, many in the financial services world have realised that they can be manipulated to ensure free, extra publicity. Coming out top – or in the leading ten – out of a hundred or more speaks volumes in customer numbers. Anyone who studies more than one best buy listing will soon realise that there can be more than one 'best.' A best buy savings account will naturally attract a lot of money. But once it does so, accountholders become victims of its success and see their rates move to the average. Financial firms need no longer be so generous as they now have enough business to keep themselves happy.

Just as record companies soon discovered how to manipulate Top 40 or 'hit parade' style sales listings to grab the free airtime publicity a chart position offers, financial companies have also been adept at using money best buys. But while music chart compilers have taken steps to curb the worst abuses, there has been little effort to control the financial fiddlers. Tables and their publication are not covered by investor protection legislation. Here are some tricks of the trade.

- Compiling self-serving tables – this has been prevalent in mortgage listings. What happens is that a mortgage broker offers a regular service to a publication. This is based not on the market as a whole but on the loans the broker wants to sell – possibly those producing the best kickbacks from lenders. Others are ignored.

- Going for the impossible – motor insurers produce tables based on mythical customers to prove they offer the lowest premiums. Some work on the basis of unlikely customers – a 17 year-old living on the Isle of Skye with a new Lamborghini, to take an extreme example. Others offer descriptions that do not include all the variables such as whether the car is garaged or if the car does not have an approved alarm system. Some home insurers have followed this line – one once featured a type of housing for a London postcode which did not exist in that area. Anyone can quote anything for non-existent risks.

- Small print. The detailed ins and outs of accounts can be difficult to explain in a simple table – let alone on radio and television. Many of the accounts featured in tables are less attractive once their hidden catches are revealed. These could include access only by slow post, penalties if more than one withdrawal is made every three or six months, and interest rates dependent on bonuses which disappear should the accountholder make a withdrawal.

- Creating loans that only those who do not need to borrow can apply for. Here the trick is to produce a chart topping personal loan where the credit scoring is so tough that only those with huge sums in the bank could possibly apply. Anyone with more modest means who actually needs a loan is then transferred to another, more expensive scheme.

- Staying out of the far less obvious world of 'worst buys' by giving bad accounts a publicity blackout. Researchers cannot probe all the deals that consumers may already have, so they concentrate on those currently on offer to new customers. One leading bank, for instance, has a poor value credit card. It has an annual fee, penalties for being one day late with payments, and a very high interest rate. But while hundreds of thousands may have the card, it does not feature on listings because it is no longer sold to new applicants.

Some of the worst excesses should be covered by the Banking Code. This lays down that banks will:

- be clear in telling customers about interest rate changes – but that depends on your reading selected newspapers for this information or logging onto the internet site. Banks do, however, send out these details by post for postal and phone accounts.
- send out once a year information on all savings accounts from that bank – better than nothing although often too late or too confusing for many customers.
- keep the interest on older, obsolete accounts (where customers are either locked into a poor value account that started out as a high interest vehicle or stay through inertia) up to other accounts with similar features. The 'weasel' word here is 'similar'. By adding in unwanted features, they can offer a lower interest rate, claiming these extras make up for the fall in income.
- reveal charges – although many will only become apparent once they have been levied. Banks can be flexible on charging and will sometimes refund penalty charges to customers who otherwise normally stay within the account rules.
- send accountholders a statement at least every three months – unless the account is rarely used when once a year is allowable.

- allow you to change a security PIN number.
- publish the bank's own complaints procedure.

The code is voluntary rather than a legal must. Policing the accounts in line with the code depends on the willingness of customers to challenge the banks with complaints. And the code itself is largely a creation of bankers eager to fend off complaints – the wording can often be woolly. Nevertheless, it is an improvement on previous practices.

Types of account

There is no obligation to have a bank account. Several million people live in a cash-only culture. But not having one can make life more difficult. Choosing the best account (or accounts, as many people have several) is a matter of looking for a deal that suits your needs.

Most accounts can be held jointly as well as by individuals. A joint account could be for a married couple, those living with a partner, or for other family relationships such as an adult who needs to help look after an aged or infirm relative or parent. Joint accounts can be accessed with one or more than one signature – it is up to those setting it up to agree at the outset. In some cases, one signature might be enough for small amounts but anything over a certain limit would demand all the parties sign.

Joint accounts mean that each signatory is responsible. A bank can legitimately pursue one of the accountholders if the other runs up a debt. It is essential to unravel a joint account if a relationship breaks up. The tax authorities view any interest from joint accounts as split equally between the holders even if the contributions from each holder are unequal. Joint accounts are less popular than they once were as the main account for a household. However, many people in a long-term relationship or who are married hold a separate joint account to pay for specified and agreed household expenses as well as their own accounts for personal spending. Both will usually pay in agreed sums each week or month.

The basic account

Banks and some building societies have introduced no-frills accounts as a response to government pressure for everyone to have an account of some description – whatever their creditworthiness. These offer direct debits so gas, electricity and phone bills can be paid without having to worry about cash or pre-payment meters. They will also allow the government to fulfil its plan to pay social security directly to recipients, and can be used by those under 18 – who are not given access to over-drafts – and by those who are fearful of running up debts.

They offer cash machine cards so withdrawals can be made up to the balance of the account. But not all have a debit card facility so some basic accounts cannot be used to pay store or restaurant bills or to book tickets by phone. Basic accounts do not allow overdrafts and most pay very low interest rates.

Chequebook or 'current' accounts

These are not designed for long-term savings but are the home to a large slice of many people's cash. Traditional advantages include instant access via cheques or cash machine or debit card, the ability to deposit cheques at a large number of locations, overdrafts if you have to borrow for a short term to tide yourself over at the end of the month, and no fees if you stay in credit. Some banks offer a 'buffer zone' so you can go £100 or so into the red without facing charges. But they normally pay virtually invisible interest rates and charge high interest on overdrafts, even higher if you do not obtain authorisation first.

Look for accounts which offer higher than average interest, or a 'sweep' facility, where money above a certain level is moved to a better paying account and 'swept' back when the main account falls to a set amount.

There are also a number of current accounts without overdrafts. These come mostly from small banks and building societies, which are eager to attract customers with substantial sums – usually £2,500 upwards. These accounts feature higher interest and, in most cases, a cheque book. However, there may be a minimum level for each cheque of between £500 and £1,000 as these accounts are not intended to replace normal current accounts but to act as a vehicle for larger sums. Some have charges when the account drops below a pre-set balance while others have fees if the number of transactions in a given period exceeds a pre-agreed level.

Passbook accounts

Passbook-based savings accounts are offered by a range of building societies and former building societies. These are primarily intended for savings but do have some bank account features. Interest rates are normally tiered – the more you have in the account, the more you earn. You can take cash out from branches or – sometimes – from cash machines. Branches will also issue cheques if there is enough money in the account. These cheques are drawn on the bank or building society. This can increase their acceptability as they will not bounce. However, they cannot be stopped once given to the recipient, although banks will cancel cheques that are lost. Passbook accounts tend to be used by older people and children. But many others use them as a separate 'rainy day' account to cope with the occasional emergency.

Other forms of savings account

Better rates tend to come from accounts operated by post, phone or Internet. These often describe themselves as 'instant access', although many will take a few days to credit a bank account with withdrawals – others limit the number of withdrawals each year. Some offer a cash machine card.

A number of these – and some passbook accounts – will pay monthly interest on a number of accounts. Most require a minimum £5,000 for this facility, although a few will start at £500. Interest rates on these accounts are lower than on similar accounts paying once or twice a year. That is to prevent people taking monthly interest and then re-investing it – otherwise this tactic would result in higher interest than the stated rate.

Notice accounts

These require anything from 30 to 180 days notice before a withdrawal can be made. In some cases, earlier withdrawal is allowed if accountholders pay an interest penalty. These are intended for larger amounts – many have a minimum – and for those who can afford to tie up cash for lengthy time spans.

Fixed rate accounts

These are also aimed at savers who are prepared to leave their money for anything between one and three years. Instead of accepting the gamble of a variable rate, savers can lock into a fixed interest rate for a set period. If interest rates fall over that time, the saver has benefited – if they rise, savers lose out. The advantage is the security offered by the fixed rate. The drawback is that money is locked into the account or bond for its life. Some allow no access; others will only return money after a steep penalty payment.

The rate on a fixed rate savings bond is set by what the money markets expect to happen over the period. A fixed rate may start off below the interest level offered on variable products because City experts expect interest rates to fall sharply.

National Savings

This is the government's savings bank, which offers a wide range of saving products – many of which are impossible to find elsewhere. Besides the variety, National Savings also guarantees complete security for your money. The government will not go bust – but if it were to do so, the country and the economy would be in such a state that all other financial products would be worthless. However in recent times many National Savings products have paid uncompetitive interest rates because the government has not needed to borrow much. The range includes:

- *Premium Bonds* – a half way house between saving and having a flutter. You cannot lose your initial money. But you swap interest for hopes of a cash prize. Nowadays you have to put a minimum £100 into the scheme. The maximum is £20,000. Once your money has been there a month, your bonds go into the monthly draw for prizes ranging from £1 million to just £50. The number of prizes is set by the interest on the total bond fund. The level varies along with other rates. But prizes are tax free. You can encash bonds at any time, subject to 8 working days notice. Overall, returns are better than the National Lottery.

- *Granny Bonds* – officially called Pensioners Guaranteed Income Bonds. Only available to those aged 60 or older. These offer a fixed rate over one, two or five years for sums from £500 to £1 million. The interest is paid monthly into a bank or building society account. It is taxable although no tax is taken at source – it is up to pensioners to pay. Holders can withdraw capital before the bonds mature – but there are costs. They must give 60 days notice during which they earn no interest or pay back 90 days worth of interest if they want immediate access.

- *Children's Bonus Bonds* – allow tax-free investments from £25 to £1,000 for children under 16 when purchased. They promise a fixed rate that lasts for five years. These appeal to grandparents but also to parents who can invest money for their offspring without affecting their own tax position. There are penalties for cashing in early.

- *Savings Certificates* – offer a tax-free fixed rate for two or five years. The interest is rolled up so there is no income. Instead, the certificate is worth more at the end of the term. There are penalties for cashing in before the two or five years are over. Savings Certificates appeal mainly to higher rate taxpayers.

- *Index-linked Certificates* – for the ultra cautious. They tend to be poor value when inflation is low but can be worthwhile if inflation takes off again. They can be bought in two or five year versions. They are similar to savings certificates except that the interest has two components. There is a low, fixed rate as the basis, and that is topped up by the rate of inflation.

- *Capital Bonds* – offer a five-year fixed interest package with the income rolled up and presented on maturity. They are taxable – taxpayers have to account each year for interest received even though they cannot use it until the bond matures.

Individual Savings Accounts (Isas)

There are tax-free versions of passbook, phone, notice, and fixed rate accounts from around 120 organisations including National Savings. These are called cash Isas (Individual Savings Accounts.) Many accounts start at £1. Whether they are bought on their own (when they are called mini cash Isas) or, more rarely, along with shares-based investments from a unit trust company (when they are called the cash component of a maxi Isa) there is an annual £3,000 savings limit per adult. Interest credited to the account does not affect this ceiling, and it grows tax-free. But while money can be withdrawn, it can never be replaced. A saver putting in £3,000 and taking out £1,000 would only be allowed to have the remaining £2,000 in that year's tax-free account. This makes them unsuitable for day to day saving. They cannot be held jointly.

The cash Isa market is competitive. You can move cash Isas between companies –but there may be transfer fees. Also watch out for tricks such as interest rate guarantees that run out in a few months, penalties for withdrawing interest, and bonus rates that disappear if you want your own money back.

Some cash Isas carry the government CAT standard mark. This stands for Charges, Access and Terms

- Charges – there must be no one-off or regular fees. Most accounts already comply with this.
- Access – you must be able to withdraw cash within 7 working days.
- Terms – the interest rate must never drop more than 2 per cent below the Bank of England base rate. Upward rate moves must be followed within a month.

AN INVESTMENT WITH A CONSCIENCE

Do you want an investment with a decent return but one that is also environmentally friendly and includes a tax break?

Friends Provident has the answer – an ISA or an Individual Saving Account. There are two types of ISAs: a Maxi or a Mini. Both allow you to shelter your investment from income and capital gains tax.

With a Maxi, you can shelter stock market investments, cash and life insurance, or a combination of these in one account, using one ISA provider.

With a Mini, you can split these three components into separate accounts and between different ISA providers.

One type of ISA is an ethical ISA, which means a company's environmental, social and ethical history is examined closely before it is invested in. Sometimes this type of fund is also known as 'light green' or 'dark green', according to the extent to which ethical and social criteria are applied.

The Friends Provident Way

Friends has a screened ethical fund called Stewardship which is very popular. Launched 17 years ago, Stewardship was the first ethical unit trust to be launched in the UK.

The Stewardship unit trust is available under the Friends ISA scheme. They all operate using stringent criteria which closely analyses a company's performance in three key areas: financial, social and environmental responsibility. This results in around 70% of the fund being invested in smaller and medium sized companies.

Firstly, an independent committee determines the Stewardship screening policy applied to key social, environmental and animal issues. Extensive research is then undertaken to ensure that before companies are invested in by Stewardship, they meet the screening criteria. This is delivered by a dedicated team of 'in house'

specialists as well as external researchers such as The Ethical Investment Research Service. Only after this detailed process is complete will a company be given the green light for investment.

Do ethical funds perform?

In the past, ethical funds have out performed their non-ethical counterparts. But it is important to remember that with any fund linked to the stock market the value of your investment can fluctuate up or down.

What sort of investment is an ISA?

Cash ISAs are usually deposit accounts offered by banks and Building Societies, although some National Savings products and cash units are also available.

Stocks and shares, is the term used for shares, bonds, gilts, unit trusts and investment trusts.

Life assurance ISAs are not very common but are usually another way of investing a lump sum linked to stock market investments.

How much can I invest?

The most is £7000 in one tax year.

How do I set up an ISA?

Ask your financial adviser about ethical ISAs. Or if you don't have a financial advisor and would like more information on Stewardship, call Friends Provident on freephone 0800 316 8415 where our efficient and professional staff will help you out.

Friends Provident Unit Trust Managers Limited is a member of Friends Provident Marketing Group and is regulated by the Personal Investment Authority and IMRO. It is also a member of the Association of Unit Trusts and Investment Funds.

FRIENDS SHARE
YOUR CONCERNS

Tax-free investment in the UK's 1ˢᵗ Ethical Fund
The Friends Provident Stewardship ISA

**The Stewardship ISA invests in the Stewardship Unit Trust,
the first of its kind in the UK. And it comes from the country's largest
ethical investment provider, with £1.3 billion of such funds under
management. With its growth of 67.8*% over the last 5 years,
you can now make a tax-free investment with a clear conscience.**

Call free or talk to your adviser
0800 316 8415
www.friendsprovident.com

FRIENDS PROVIDENT

However, the CAT standard mark is not a government guarantee, and does not necessarily indicate best value.

Investing it

Taking a risk

Once you have enough money to pay your way and a reserve in your savings and other non-risk accounts, you can consider yourself an investor. Investing involves making decisions – deciding to do nothing and leaving all your money in a safe bank account should be seen as a decision. But most investors attempt to make better returns from their spare cash than they can obtain in the bank or building society – and that involves taking risks. Over the years investors have increasingly turned to the stock market for these extra returns. Here are some basic pointers.

- You have to speculate to accumulate – unless you are prepared to take higher risks with your money, you will have no chance of making a greater return than the typical 'safe investment'.
- Market forces are powerful – the value of shares and other investment assets can change dramatically over a short time
- No one knows the future – no matter how confident they may seem. Investment analysts, financial advisers and other 'experts' often merely repeat what others tell them.
- Amateurs can often do as well as professionals – even if they pick investments with a pin.
- All advice comes with an 'agenda' – usually to sell a financial product. Investment analysts are in business to sell shares; financial advisers, whether independent or not, make their money by selling insurance bonds and unit trusts.
- Putting all your eggs in one financial basket is very foolhardy.
- Spreading your risks through diversification is always better.
- Investment should be for the long term – over years and decades shares and products based on shares tend to do best.

Financial advice for changing situations.

As the oldest clearing bank in the UK, we're well used to managing change. So however your situation changes, Bank of Scotland Investors Club can help you make the most of it. Our Financial Planning Consultants are on hand to offer advice whenever and wherever it suits you: at your local branch, in your home, or at your workplace.

Either way we are here to help. For more information or to arrange an appointment, call us on **0845 600 4488** quoting reference CLBO1102 or visit our website at www.bankofscotland.uk/investorsclub

❈ BANK OF SCOTLAND
Investors Club

- Trying to spot the tops and bottoms of share price movements is impossible.
- Investors too often buy when the price has already increased because advisers and financial companies like to boast about gains already made.
- Investors often sell after the price has collapsed.
- The past is no indicator of the future.
- Investors cannot have both huge capital gains and huge income from assets – one is a play-off against the other.

These points are mostly negative – purposely so. The history of asset-backed or risk investment is full of instances of people being lured into losses that they cannot afford by smooth-talking financial salespeople. Many first-time investors were persuaded to put money into technology unit trusts by greedy investment companies and the overall hype surrounding the Internet boom in early 2000.

The firms played heavily on the easiest line to peddle to first-timers and the gullible – prices have already doubled or trebled or quadrupled. Therefore, the implication went, they will continue to do so. The minority who asked why a company with the turnover of a corner shop should be worth £1billion were fobbed off. The world had changed, said the experts.

Like all other bubbles, it was a case of 'emperor's new clothes'. Within months, these hapless investors had lost half or even more of their money. This is fine if investors fully understood the risks but most will have been attracted by adverts showing share price graphs pointing upwards like a rocket with the risk factors in the tiniest typeface. But the technology bubble – and the Japanese bubble of the late 1980s when the main Japanese phone company was worth more than the entire German stockmarket – are the exceptions that prove the rule. A well spread portfolio of shares should, over time, beat other forms of investment and savings.

Most people are investors whether they know it or not. Their endowment policies and pension funds are invested in the stock market. Despite spectacular crashes, overall the stock market has offered better returns than leaving money in the bank. But it has to be with money that you can afford to leave tied up for a long time and which you are ultimately prepared to lose.

Many people sort out their own risk-based investments – arguably they have as much chance of getting it right as so-called experts and advisers. They need, however, to take a leaf out of the advisers' book. Advisers have to conduct a fact-find before recommending investments on an individual basis under investor protection rules although, oddly, this necessity does not apply if they send out information such as junk mail (even if the letter appears personalised) or in adverts. You should consider factors such as:

- what you are actually investing for, what is the timescale and amount required – and is it realistic?
- your disposable income and that of your partner if any – it is only spare cash that should be invested. Knowing how much you have available can also determine the form of investment you make – some are more suitable for those with larger or smaller amounts
- the tax position of you and your partner – some investments are best suited for non-taxpayers; others for higher rate payers.
- retirement planning – your lifestyle needs such as when you hope to retire and what pension you can count on can make a big difference to the investments that might be suitable for you.
- your age – the younger you are, the less you may have to spare but the more time you have to let it grow.
- your attitude to risk – you may be prepared to take a gamble but not a 100–1 bet on the ultra-outsider.

The stock market

Most investments including shares are based on the stock market. Around one in five people already own shares – possibly in privatised companies such as BT, British Gas, or a water or electricity company.

Get off to a flying start ...

Whether you've already got just a few shares ... perhaps from privatisation issues like BT and Railtrack, or from when your building society converted to a plc, like the Halifax or Abbey National,

have built up a larger portfolio, maybe with shares from your employer or established from investing over time ...

or are just starting out, we make it easy for you to buy, sell and manage your investments, with dealing commission from just £2.50

From a Share Account giving you ready access to your portfolio by telephone, post and on-line 24 hours a day, and the ability to buy or sell quickly, easily and at low cost ...

to a **Self-Select Share ISA**, for tax-free growth and the ability to choose the shares you want to meet your personal investment aims ...

transferring your existing **PEPs** into one easy to manage fund, giving you direct control so you avoid the risk of holding the same investments in different funds, managed by different people ...

and **informed, independent, impartial advice** that will help you choose the right shares, decide when's best to buy or sell and provide a friendly ear for when you want another view on your own investment ideas ... you'll find The Share Centre has all the answers you need.

Find out how we can help you make the most of your investments ... visit **www.share.com** or call us free on **0800 800 008**

The
Share Centre
Helping you make the most of your investments

Others hold shares in financial companies such as Halifax or Friends Provident, which have turned from being customer owned companies (known as mutuals) to shareholder owned concerns. These shares were given away in the form of windfalls.

If you work for a big company that is quoted on the stock market you will probably have the chance of investing in that firm's shares through Save As You Earn (Saye) schemes or company share option plans. Both these employee share plans are designed to give you an each way bet – if the shares prosper you gain, but if they fall you can walk away without a loss.

Saye involves signing up for a monthly sum from £5 to £250 for three, five or seven years. When the plan matures, there is a bonus – effectively interest. That money can then be used to buy the company shares at a discount of between 10 to 20 per cent under their market value. Alternatively, savers can just take the cash.

Options work in a similar fashion. The company offers employees a number of shares at a future date at a discount to today's prices. When the option date arrives, employees can either buy the shares at the set value – or walk away. There are a number of schemes available to companies.

However, whether paid for, sold at a discount, or free, shares can go up and down. This gives the stock market the – sometimes richly deserved – reputation of being a casino. But if you are careful and patient, you can win. You will not make spectacular overnight returns unless you are simply lucky enough to be in the right place at the right time. Instead, aim for a few percentage points each year more than the return on risk-free investments. Those small gains mount up over longer periods. Put £1,000 in the bank at 3 per cent and, assuming you leave the interest to compound, you will have £2,000 in around 24 years. A stock market investment growing at 6 per cent would be worth £4,000 over the same period.

Companies on the stock market are divided up into 'shares' – billions in the case of the largest firms. You can buy just one share in a company or many thousands if you can afford it. All shares follow the

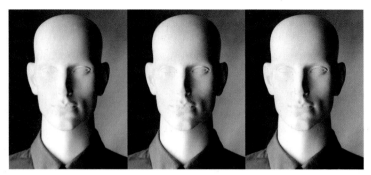

Not all discount brokers are created equal

 When you deal with Janice Thomson at Moneygro you will soon notice the difference. For instance, charging a flat fee of just £12.50 for unit trust transaction. Simply the lowest cost to be found anywhere. As well as unit trusts, you will find our Triple Bonus ISA and PEP consolidation service equally competitive and efficient. It offers hundreds of top funds with discounts of up to 5%, low cost fund switching and an annual cash loyalty bonus.

So if you are in the market for unit trusts, ISAs or PEP transfers contact Janice Thomson. You will find the experience refreshingly different.

For more information call our freephone number, or send us an e-mail.

m o n e y g r o . l t d

SIMPLY MORE CHOICE

Moneygro Limited, FREEPOST, LON 17217,
15 Landford Road, London SW15 1ZZ

Freephone: 0800 1695745

www.moneygro.com   e-mail: janice@moneygro.com

same principles of supply and demand. When investors like the company, the number of those wanting to buy exceeds those wanting to sell, so demand forces up the price. Equally, if stock market participants are unhappy about a company, there will be more sellers around than buyers so the price falls.

You can invest in just one company, but unless you want to take a gamble with individual shares experts say it is better to spread your money around a basket of investments. You can do this yourself by buying a number of individual shares. You will, however, need time, patience, the inclination – and at least £50,000 to £100,000 in spare cash to make this worthwhile.

Most money from private individuals goes into the stock market through unit trusts, open-ended investment companies (OEICs) and investment trusts. All of these offer a basket – or 'fund' – of shares, and sometimes other assets, for those prepared to put in very small sums. Some will accept £250 as a minimum lump sum – or as little as £20 if you agree to pay in each month into a savings scheme.

Unit trusts and OEICs are much the same as far as investors are concerned, although there are legal differences. Many unit trusts are being converted into OEICs. Newspapers and magazines tend to refer to both as 'unit trusts'. There are around 1,600 to choose from. The money you pay in goes, after deducting an upfront charge to pay commission to sellers and costs to the investment company, straight into buying shares. If the fund was previously worth £10m and you invest £10,000 after costs, it now has £10,010,000 to buy shares. But if investors decide to pull out, the fund shrinks.

You are directly backing the skills of the fund managers to buy and sell investments in line with the label on the trust. If it says 'Japan', it should buy and sell stocks in that country – a 'small company' fund should concentrate on stock market tiddlers, selling them if they become giants.

Tracker funds are trusts that buy all the shares in a stock market index in their correct proportions – they will hold 5 per cent of their portfolio in a firm that constitutes 5 per cent of the market index, 2 per cent in a company whose involvement in the index is 2 per cent of the total, and so on. This takes out human judgement as these funds can be run by computer. Tracker trusts will never top tables nor will they appear in the fourth division. Taking out the humans also takes out costs – tracker funds typically charge unit holders 0.5 per cent a year – others are usually three times as much. Saving 1 per cent a year does not seem much – leave it for ten years on a £10,000 sum and, all other factors being equal, you have around £1,000 more.

Investment trusts often work on lower charges with a good number of these funds only taking between 0.15 per cent to 0.5 per cent a year. But it is not just charges that differentiate them from the far more heavily marketed unit trusts. They have a different structure.

Investment trusts are themselves companies quoted on the stock market that invest in the shares of other trading companies like Next or Marks & Spencer, British Telecom or Cable & Wireless. The main effect of this is that the trust's own shares do not always directly reflect the value of the underlying investments – the trust's shares can trade at a discount or a premium and this can vary over time. This in turn can enhance gains or boost losses for investors.

How to choose a fund

The first decision is; 'What do I want from my investment?' The main choices are:

- going all out for capital growth – look for trusts that pay little or nothing in the way of dividends. This is often a suitable option for those with many years before they will need the money.
- looking for some income and some capital growth. There are funds that offer a balance between the two. The income should grow over time.
- seeking income – usually a choice for the retirement years where the main interest is boosting a pension with a regular, high income. These trusts are unlikely to offer much growth in capital or in income.

Most funds concentrate on a country such as the United Kingdom, Japan or the United States, on a region – Europe, the Pacific, Latin America, or a theme such as technology, healthcare or small companies. Some, including most of the big investment trusts, take a worldwide approach. This does not tie the managers down – equally it can be difficult to see what you have bought. There are also funds that invest in bonds – effectively loans made to companies or governments.

Selecting the country or theme is the first essential. Over the past five years, you could have lost money in the average Japanese fund but made good profits in the United States. But remember the past is no guide to the future – the next five years could see that trend continuing or the exact opposite or any one of an infinity of other combinations.

Less critical is selecting the fund management company. While a few outperform dramatically, usually by taking higher risks and getting it right, only one in a hundred does well year after year.

The value of the individual fund manager is also debatable. Some funds have slumped when a 'superstar' manager leaves. Others continue as though nothing had changed. There are no certainties in investment. While fund companies say 'look at my past record' with little justification, arguably the only ones where investors should look at the previous performance is in filtering out the worst.

Financial advisers and fund companies depend on selling unit trusts for their earnings. With the exception of advisers who work for fees relating to the time they take with you rather than depending on commissions, only the most honest will tell you to stay away and leave your money in the bank or building society.

There is a growing interest in 'ethical' or 'green' funds. Most filter out companies in areas that investors want to shun – typically tobacco manufacturers, armaments makers, firms that deal with dictatorships, or are involved in animal testing, pornography or the exploitation of children. Shares in companies that harm the environment are also on the negative list. Others – known as 'best of class' ethical funds work on the premise of encouraging companies. They buy shares in the oil company or electricity supplier that has made the most progress in moving over to renewable energy; or in the pharmaceutical firm that has gone furthest in replacing animal testing; or in the sports goods maker that is trying the hardest to replace child labour. These funds also balance off positive factors. A supermarket will get minus points for selling tobacco but plus points for charitable or community work.

Ethical investment proponents say their funds represent more than just conscience-salving or lifestyle investing. They say companies that comply with their rules are more likely to be forward looking and, hence, a better bet for the future.

How to buy funds

Unit trusts are sold by companies directly through adverts and mailshots, through 'fund supermarkets' and via independent financial advisers (IFAs). Going direct to the fund management company is usually the least sensible method. You will only be able to buy that firm's own range – and you will probably pay the full price, which includes the 3 per cent commission paid to advisers even though you have had little or no advice.

Fund supermarkets are a new idea where you can buy from a choice of around 500 unit trusts by post, phone or Internet, using a bank debit card for payments. Fund supermarkets have the advantage that you can keep a variety of trusts managed by different investment companies in one account. This can be useful to check on your overall holdings – the supermarket will have a valuation facility – and will save time when sending in details of your investments and any dividends to the Inland Revenue. The funds are sold at a discount to the full purchase cost, typically of between 3 to 5 per cent.

Buying through an independent financial adviser (IFA) gives further choice and the ability to negotiate a discount on the upfront or 'initial' charge. If you have substantial sums – from £20,000 upwards – the adviser might construct a portfolio of trusts so you spread your money around even further. Only a few specialist advisers are competent to do this. Most will simply suggest 'flavour of the month' trusts. These are funds that are heavily marketed at that time by fund management companies. The evidence of the past is that these trusts are best avoided – by the time the message has turned into a fund and it has been launched and marketed, the original reasoning for the out-performance may well have become stale.

Independent financial advisers are supposed to work in customers' interests and come up with 'best advice'. But that rule often ceases to apply when they publish 'investment guides', often sent out by post or circulated with publications. Here, their recommendations can be decided by which fund company is prepared to pay them towards the costs of the guide. They are often, but not always, a collection of advertisements masquerading as independent advice.

Cashing in a unit trust is easy – you do this directly with the management company. There is no charge for selling.

Investment trust shares can be bought through stockbrokers for a fee, but most smaller investors buy them through low cost savings schemes run by the fund management company. A typical plan will offer a choice of a lump sum investment (from £250) or monthly contributions (usually from £50 but some are as little as £20). You have to pay the 0.5 per cent government stamp duty on each purchase but after that the costs are tiny – far less than a unit trust or going through a stockbroker.

Monthly plans are operated with direct debits from a bank account – but there are no penalties for stopping, missing a month, decreasing the payment or deciding to pay more. One advantage of a regular savings plan is that you do not need to make a 'market timing' decision. Instead of trying to second guess good and bad times, a task that routinely defeats the professionals, the money goes in each month. When stock markets are high, your money buys fewer shares; when it falls, your money purchases more. You can sell whenever you want – usually on the same low cost terms through the plan. Unit trust companies also have regular savings schemes.

Stocks and shares Isas

Stockmarket Isas are, in most cases, simply an investment fund in a tax-free form. These so-called stocks and shares Isas can invest in virtually all unit and investment trusts – with income and capital gains exempt from tax. 'Tax free' investing is a powerful marketing tool, but check up what the saving will be before investing. On some trusts such as those investing in the Far East or the United States, dividends are low or non-existent so your annual savings might be counted in pennies. But on high yielding bond funds, the income tax savings can be substantial, especially for higher rate taxpayers.

Few investors pay capital gains tax – there is an annual allowance (currently £7,800) per person. But tax freedom could be valuable in the future if your selection performs well. In addition, you do not have to report Isa holdings on tax forms.

You can invest up to £7,000 a year into funds through a 'maxi' stocks and shares Isa (which precludes you having a cash Isa) or £3,000 into a 'mini' stocks and shares Isa. The money usually goes into one fund, or funds from the same management company. But you can 'mix and match' further by using a fund supermarket. You can also put individual shares into an Isa through one of the schemes operated by stockbrokers.

Buying shares

At the height of the dotcom bubble, it seemed that every second person was wheeling and dealing in shares online. Some appeared to make huge fortunes – at least on paper. But the real money is never there until you sell.

Getting involved in individual shares demands lifestyle decisions. Do you want to be an active investor? This can entail moving in and out of the market, often backing shares for just a short time. To do this, you will need to invest heavily with your own personal time as well. Researching shares can be long-winded; you will need a good internet search ability to pick up information and also judge what other investors are doing through 'chat rooms', although chat room participants are not necessarily right in their judgements. Some use the net to 'pump'n'dump' They exaggerate the potential of a share that they hold to suck in new investors, create demand, and force the price up – all so they can sell their holding at a profit. You may also need a lifestyle that enables you to buy and sell shares during stock market trading hours. That rules out many at work, but it is suited to retired people.

Most individual share investors use 'execution only' Internet brokers. They receive no advice from their brokers, who are only involved in buying and selling. Some web sites let investors set up dummy portfolios so they can test out their theories first, at no cost, before trying for real. You can also look at charts of share price ups and downs; some investors believe that 'charting' helps them predict the future, others say this is rubbish.

Stockbroking costs are lower thanks to the Internet but frequent trading can be expensive – all those one per cents or £20 flat fees add up – and you still have to pay 0.5 per cent stamp duty on purchases.

If individual share buying does attract you, here are some tips for making money.

- What is the state of the stock market? Is the index of leading shares (the Footsie in the UK, the Dow Jones in the US) rising (a bull market) or falling (a bear market)? In a bull phase, most shares tend to rise; in a bear market, only a few will resist selling pressure and avoid falls.
- Am I investing in growth? Look around to see if the company's products are likely to increase or decrease in importance or stay the same. Common sense is useful – there are only so many mobile phones or computers people can own, after which sales depend on replacements for broken or very outdated models. People tend to adopt new technologies gradually – unless they are sold at very low prices. Are health clubs a gimmick or a permanent feature of life? Will people continue to drink beer? Or buy food at supermarkets?

- Is the activity profitable? Share prices ultimately depend on dividends, which need profits. Companies can make losses for a time but they need good reasons, such as investing in new premises or machinery or nursing a market that will soon grow.

- What does the company do to differentiate itself from competitors? Is it better? Does it have new ideas?

- Is all this 'in the price'? You will be up against full time investment professionals who have access to at least as much information as you have. By the time you get to know a fact, others in the market may have acted already on it so your knowledge is less valuable.

- Avoid 'tip sheets' – expensive subscription services that purport to predict winners. These sell themselves on the quality of their past advice. They select their success stories and ignore their flops. Some adopt a 'scatter gun' approach – they tip so many that some are almost bound to go up.

4
Money and Property

Virtually everyone wants to own property, so they say. But in reality, home buying is not for all, all the time. House prices have been rising strongly over recent years, doubling in some parts of the country – and when that happened before, in the late 1980s, many people so mortgaged themselves up to the hilt that they had no financial leeway when interest rates rose or when a relationship broke down, or when redundancy hit. The result was hundreds of thousands losing their home as lenders pulled the plug. They could not even sell many of the flats they had worked so hard to buy, while even the more desirable properties plunged in value.

Lenders, estate agents, property developers and anyone else whose job depends on home sales, have all been saying – as they did a decade or so ago – that it won't happen again. 'It's not the same this time' is the most dangerous phrase in the financial lexicon. So rule number one of buying property is that a home is for nesting, not investing.

Look on home purchase as a long-term affair. You need a property that will cover your needs for many years – and you should only buy one in partnership with someone else if you are sure your relationship will last. Flitting from flat to flat every time you see prices rise can be physically and mentally exhausting. And it's expensive, as each move can cost thousands in estate agency bills, stamp duty, legal expenses, survey fees, and the cash involved in the moving process. Like much else, you can add hefty percentages on to your original cost estimate to get the real picture.

If you are not ready for settling down or you feel home buying could stretch your finances, rent instead. A significant minority do this – some out of choice, some because social housing is more in line with their income and spending patterns, and others because they are saving up for a deposit on a property.

Renters do not need a formal credit check so there will be no problems if you do not have a settled job – renting is ideal for those setting out on self employment or on short-term contract work. Nor will you need to pay legal, survey and other moving costs or – usually – insurance on the property itself. Repairs to the property are the landlord's responsibility, although most landlords insist on keeping back a month's rent in case of damage caused by tenants.

There are a growing number of properties to rent including housing association properties for those on moderate earnings and a large number of homes purchased by 'buy to let' investors. So the selection is greater than it once was. Landlords usually want only a six-month commitment, so you can walk away from the deal relatively easily if something goes wrong.

Those advocating buying say it is essential to get a foot on the housing purchase ladder – but it is easier to fall off a ladder than to climb one. Buying makes sense for the majority in the longer run, though only if they can be sure that they have factored in the problems and setbacks that hit all too many home purchasers in the late 1980s.

The rest of this chapter is concerned with buying, financing and selling a property.

Buying a home

This is the biggest financial transaction that most people ever undertake. So don't even look at an estate agent's window until you are sure how much you can afford.

To work this out, first see how much you can borrow. If you are single, multiply your annual salary by 3.25 times. You may find that some lenders will use a higher figure – often 4 and even up to 5 or 6 times. These bigger ratios can be either for the good reason that your career has a clear and fast earnings progression or for the bad reason that the bank needs to lend more. For couples where the partner earns much less, the lender may just add one times the second salary to the limit for the main wage earner.

Alternatively, where partners buying a house have similar incomes, lenders will multiply the joint earnings by around 2.5 to 2.75 times. They will tend to use whichever formula enables them to lend more.

On the basis of a standard ratio of 3.25 times the sole or higher salary plus one times the lower salary or 2.5 times joint earnings – whichever is the higher, here are some figures. A couple earning £25,000 and £12,000 would get £93,250 (3.25 × £25,000 plus £12,000) by the first formula or £92,500 (£25,000 plus £12,000 × 2. 5) with the second. A couple earning £30,000 and £20,000 would get £117,500 by the first formula but £125,000 by the second.

Some home loan companies will adjust these figures to take account of any other substantial debts you may have. Different lenders and mortgage brokers could all come up with different ratios so it is worthwhile for anyone seeking to maximise their mortgage potential to ask several.

Most lenders are happy to consider non-marital (including same sex) relationships. Whether you are single, living with a partner, gay, straight or married is unlikely to make any difference – the basic rule is that lenders will want the name of anyone whose earnings are counted to appear on the mortgage paperwork.

Now add any lump sum savings you might have available or expected profit after you sell your present home and repay the mortgage (deduct any loss). The result is the amount you have available for home purchase. This is not the same as the sum you can afford to pay for a house because it has to include the costs and expenses associated with moving. As a rule of thumb, allow 5 to 8 per cent for this on most houses. But in London and the South East, you will need to add in more.

Properties costing £60,000 and under attract no stamp duty. Between £60,001 and £250,000, there is a 1 per cent charge – levied on the entire amount and not just that above £60,000. At £250,000 to £500,000, the duty rises to 3 per cent – again on the whole sum – while at £500,000 and upwards, the tax is 4 per cent.

Your creditworthiness

Lenders will verify the earnings figures you give them with your employer. Ask your prospective mortgage company about how it treats extra payments such as overtime, bonuses and commissions. Some lenders will ignore part or all of these if they are large or irregular.

Home loan companies will also check credit ratings through organisations such as Equifax or Experian. There is no obligation to lend anyone anything and they may refuse a loan if you have county court judgements (sheriff's court judgements in Scotland), have moved home or job several times in a short period, are not on the electoral register, have been bankrupt, or have had other debt problems. If you are turned down, always ask why. Errors can occur and there may be special mortgage schemes for those with difficulties. Lenders impose special conditions for the self employed and those on short-term contracts. They might be high earners, but lenders do not trust their staying power. Most will only lend to those running their own businesses if they can produce three years' worth of accountant audited figures to back up their earnings claims. Those with short-term contracts have to show continuity of employment to qualify.

There are two ways ahead for those who fail these tests. One route is the higher cost loan designed for the 'credit-impaired'. The interest rate is set above normal levels to cover the extra risk, but after a time – usually three years – the buyer can return to standard rate loans provided the payments have been maintained. Interest rates vary according to the credit record – someone who has been bankrupt will pay more.

A second avenue is the 'self certification' loan. Here buyers tell lenders what they can afford. It is suitable for older people who have built up savings that produce investment income, and for those who can afford to put down a substantial deposit – home loan companies insist on a minimum 20 to 30 per cent down payment to provide a cushion for them if the purchaser fails to pay.

How long should the mortgage be?

Traditionally virtually all mortgages were set at 25 years. Most still are. But there is no reason why they should be. The 25-year stretch had two advantages. The longer the loan lasted, the more inflation and rising earnings could wipe out much of the repayments in real terms. A £10,000 loan in 1976 would have been around three to four times typical earnings. By 2001, it was less than half average salaries. The monthly payments started off as a substantial sum and ended up as little more than the cost of an evening out. At the same time, the endowment mortgage repayment method needed a full 25 years to work. It was smart to owe money.

Now both those reasons have disappeared. Assuming inflation remains low, there will be no rising prices riding to the rescue of borrowers – and the endowment mortgage has been largely discredited. It now makes sense to pay off a loan as soon as possible consistent with affordability. The extra monthly cost of paying over shorter periods is relatively small, the savings from early repayment are large.

Repaying £100,000 at 7 per cent:

- over 25 years = £706.78 a month (total £212,034)
- over 20 years = £775.30 a month (total £186,072)
- over 15 years = £898.83 a month (total £161,789)
- over 10 years = £1,161.08 a month (total £139,330)

Older people may wish to repay as quickly as possible – they may be able to afford this if children have left home. And many will want to repay their mortgage while they are still working so their retirement years are free of loan payments. Not paying a mortgage can help bridge the gap between the purchasing power of a salary and that of a retirement income.

Legalistics

Couples, whether gay or straight, need to come to their own arrangements over sharing the bills and paying the loan. But where more than one person is involved, the law takes a hand. Two or more people can own property in two ways.

'Joint tenants' is the usual method used by married couples or long-term partners. Here they both own the whole property jointly. If one dies, the home automatically becomes the sole property of the survivor. This cannot be undone through a will.

'Tenants in common' is more akin to owning shares in a company. Here, the interests of each partner are fixed at the outset – it could be 50/50 or 70/30 for two people or 25/25/25/25 if four people are buying jointly – whatever the buyers agree. If one buyer dies, the share can be left in a will. Or it could be sold on to another person. This form of ownership is better suited to relationships that may not last.

But however a property is legally held, everyone named on the property paperwork is responsible for paying the mortgage even if their share is low. Where one partner walks away from the debt or is unable to pay, the other (or others) have to pay and can be chased for money owing.

Loan to value percentage

This is mortgage company speak for the proportion of the purchase price which is backed by their lending. It is the inverse of the deposit. A £100,000 home purchased with a £20,000 deposit produces an LTV of 80 per cent (100 per cent less the 20 per cent lump sum).

The lower the LTV, the happier the lender. If a buyer defaults on payment, the lender is less exposed as the buyer has more cash value in the property, which can be grabbed. But borrowers also benefit from a low LTV. Small deposits (or high LTVs) narrow the range of mortgages on offer. Many lenders increase interest rates for customers who can only put down a small deposit – this is an alternative to the older practice of charging a lump sum Mortgage Indemnity Guarantee (Mig insurance) for high LTVs. Loans offering 100 per cent LTVs do exist, although they are normally noticeably more expensive.

Which mortgage?

Newspapers, including the *Daily Express*, routinely carry 'best buy' mortgage tables, which show the loans with the lowest interest rates. So how come anyone else sells any mortgages? Why should a buyer pay more?

One reason could be that buyers do not know they could find cheaper deals. Banks and building societies rarely sell loans other than their own-label mortgages. They will simply not tell you about better deals elsewhere. Mortgage brokers may not always help either. They may want to sell their own 'exclusive' arrangements, which may, or may not, be better than those on offer elsewhere. And they are under no obligation to look at the entire market – even if they are part of a firm offering 'independent financial advice.' But there is another reason why finding the best value mortgage can be difficult. Mortgages rarely come in plain vanilla – more often they have many different bells and whistles that comparing one with another is virtually impossible. For instance, a mortgage with a 3 per cent discount will obviously look more attractive in tables than one with a 1 per cent discount. But if the 3 per cent discount only lasts three months and the 1 per cent saving had a three-year life, the latter would be better value. It would also produce less of a 'payment shock' when the discount ended.

Fixed rates, whether help is offered with legal and other costs, compulsory insurances, LTVs, early repayment penalties and a whole host of other variables all serve to muddy the waters. What appears cheap now may turn out to be expensive later.

The mortgage maze

Once over the credit check hurdle, decide how you intend repaying. Mortgage brokers may have a wider variety of home loans than a bank or building society but you may either have to pay a fee or buy potentially expensive or unwanted insurance. Brokers cannot charge more than a token amount if they fail to find you a suitable loan. Never pay fees up front.

Financial advice for changing situations.

As the oldest clearing bank in the UK, we're well used to managing change. So however your situation changes, Bank of Scotland Investors Club can help you make the most of it. Our Financial Planning Consultants are on hand to offer advice whenever and wherever it suits you: at your local branch, in your home, or at your workplace.

Either way we are here to help. For more information or to arrange an appointment, call us on **0845 600 4488** quoting reference CLBO1102 or visit our website at www.bankofscotland.uk/investorsclub

⊗ BANK OF SCOTLAND
Investors Club

These are the main types of home loans:

- *Capital repayment* – you pay interest and repay part of the loan each month. As the mortgage progresses, the interest portion decreases while capital repayments increase. The advantage is simplicity and the certainty you will complete the mortgage. You may also be able to stretch or shrink the loan period. The repayment method can be used with fixed, capped and discounted loans. The main drawback is that early payments consist largely of interest so little will be repaid in the first years.

- *Interest only* – pay interest to the lender on a monthly basis with a separate investment – endowment, Individual Savings Account or pension – that should pay off the capital by the end of the loan term. Overall, monthly payments may be lower; your investment could outpace the interest rate so you can either shorten the repayment period or have a lump sum at the end; and you could benefit from tax savings on pensions or Isas. But there are disadvantages. There is no guarantee that an investment will grow sufficiently to pay off the loan – you might have to increase payments or face a shortfall. Your investment flexibility could be constrained – you can only have one stocks and shares Isa in any year – while personal or stakeholder pension contributions used for home purchase cut back on your future retirement income.

- *Flexible mortgages* – these are similar to capital repayment mortgages but you can vary payments – providing you adhere to a minimum schedule – and pay extra lump sums without penalty. Borrowers can overpay to decrease the loan period – even relatively small extra amounts can cut years from the term. But they can also take payment holidays, underpay, and withdraw lump sums in some circumstances. Flexible mortgages are usually more popular with second and subsequent time buyers – perhaps couples who no longer have children to take care of – and those with uneven earnings. The main advantages are the interest saved by faster loan repayment; the ability to overpay with occasional extra payments such as bonuses and overtime; payment holidays; and, in some schemes, borrowing back from any growth in the value of your property. But there are drawbacks. Interest rates can be higher and discounts less generous, while there are few fixed or capped loans so you do not have that rate security. A variant is to link a flexible mortgage with a current account to maximise interest savings.

Insurance

Lenders usually require life insurance to repay the mortgage if you or your partner dies. Some may waive this if you have sufficient life cover elsewhere. Life cover is built into endowment policies. Some borrowers also take out 'critical illness' cover. This pays a lump sum if policyholders suffer life-threatening conditions such as strokes, cancer or heart attacks.

Optional accident, sickness and unemployment (ASU) cover takes care of monthly mortgage payments if your earnings cease for one of these reasons. The payments usually continue for a maximum of two years. Help with your mortgage payments from Income Support is means-tested, only covers a proportion of most payments, and normally has a nine-month waiting period.

Finding a home

Once you have found a property that fits your needs and budget, make an offer – usually through the estate agent. This is not legally binding in England and Wales (the system in Scotland is different) so you can pull out if surveys or legal searches produce problems, if finance falls through, or if you change your mind. But equally, an accepted offer does not bind the vendor.

Sellers may accept or reject offers immediately, but agents often advise waiting for further interest – especially if the property has not been long on the market. Always ask the seller's agent what is happening if you hear nothing after a week. Your offer depends on:

- the state of the market – when prices are rising strongly, pitch your offer at or near the asking price. There could be several rival offers. But in a slow or falling market, your initial offer could be lower.
- comparability – judge whether the asking price is high or low by looking at other similar properties.
- why the vendor wants to move – some have urgent reasons (work, or family needs) and might accept a lower price.
- your own position – most vendors are realistic and expect bargaining. You strengthen your hand if you have finance in place – a lender's certificate to show they have approved a loan in principle; cash in the bank; or your existing home already has a purchaser. This gives the vendor confidence that you will be able to complete on time.

Once you have made a firm offer, the vendor's agent will ask you for details of your lawyer to progress the purchase. You could be 'gazumped' when your offer is thrown out for a better proposal. Or, when prices are falling, you might reduce your own offer – known as 'gazundering'.

Part of the house buying process involves looking at fixtures and fittings, and considering their value. Few homes, other than a few ware-house conversions, are sold as empty shells. Fixtures are items that cannot be removed without damaging the property and, often, rendering it uninhabitable. They include lavatories, radiators, gas pipes, and electrical wiring. Fittings include curtain rails, built in bookcases, TV aerials, wall lights, fitted carpets, and even the toilet paper holder. These can be removed causing little damage. Other items such as free standing cookers, fridges, curtains, light bulbs and removable garden sheds may also be included in the sale if both sides agree.

What is included – or excluded – beyond essential fixtures can be contentious and negotiable. The law is often unclear – and going to court is rarely worth it. Both parties should establish, on a room-by-room basis, fittings and free-standing items that are part of the sale and what will be removed. Agreement can then be reached on items to be left. This may lead to haggling.

Include everything in the fixtures and fittings schedule – down to light bulbs. Moving in and finding no light bulbs is not a financial disaster –

just a nuisance. Equally, do not pay top prices for an old stove or washing machine. Always set agreed prices down in writing and ensure your solicitor receives a copy of the full schedule of fixtures and fittings.

Negotiating some items separately can sometimes reduce stamp duty. Stamp duty has trigger points where the rate goes up – and not just on the balance, but on the whole sum.

To take a simple example: agree £60,500 for a property and you pay 1 per cent stamp duty on the entire sum – £605. But splitting the price into the property at £59,900 and £600 for fittings cuts out this tax as the property is now under the £60,000 stamp duty starting level. These valuations must be realistic – the Inland Revenue can check.

Chains

Chains can affect all but first-time buyers and cash buyers. They occur because the purchaser in transaction A is dependent on money from buyer B who is waiting for the purchaser in transaction C and so on. A, B and C can only buy if they sell existing properties. If one link breaks, the whole chain collapses.

Some agents and new home developers repair broken chains by buying the home whose purchase has fallen through, usually at lower than the asking price.

Scotland

Property in Scotland usually sells on the basis of 'offers over' and a closing date. However, new properties are generally sold by developers at a fixed price.

Once you have found a property, tell your solicitor who will 'note interest' on your behalf. The solicitor may help in suggesting how much over the minimum price you should bid, and with negotiations on 'moveables' – anything that is not firmly fixed to the property. Once an offer is accepted, it is a binding contract under Scottish law.

5
Household Finances

Getting married or living together

Talking about money sounds like the least romantic thing that star struck lovers could do. But no couple – whatever the style of their relationship – can avoid the imperatives of cash. Arguments and problems over money are the underlying cause of the majority of marriage and partnership breakdowns. Few people arrange their finances in the expectation they will separate or divorce. However it is possible to sort out your money in such a way that both parties can protect themselves in the event of the relationship ending. English law does not recognise 'prenuptial' agreements of the type popular in Hollywood, but marriage puts an end to a number of contracts – it makes wills invalid, for instance.

Before embarking on a partnership, both sides should be aware of the other's personal balance sheet – their earnings, assets and debts. Just how much privacy or independence each wants is then a matter of personal choice so each couple can come to their own arrangements. But if you decide to have total privacy one from the other – and some do – then it is better that this is discussed early on in the relationship and agreed upon rather than cause rows and upsets later on. It is obviously best to know at the outset if one of you is a total skinflint and the other a complete spendthrift.

Once you have taken the decision to live as a couple and have at least a degree of financial inter-dependence, then you can embark on joint financial planning. You may both have your own savings, pensions, bank accounts and investments – but there could well be areas where looking at your money as a whole enables you to make the best out of what you have. Completely relying on your partner – unless you absolutely have to – is nothing less than foolhardy. It would leave you vulnerable in the event of a relationship breakdown.

Under present laws, anyone embarking on any relationship other than a heterosexual marriage, has no automatic legal rights in a relationship. The law does not recognise gay couples, while different sex partnerships outside of marriage can also present difficulties. But the sheer numbers of those in these relationships has already changed attitudes.

One solution for non-married couples is to draw up a form of contract. Even if there is no intention to go to court, a document helps set out both sides' responsibilities. It is easier to keep to a decision on who pays the mortgage or rent, the utility bills, the supermarket tally and all the other expenses of daily living and how the costs of these will be apportioned, if there is an agreement at the outset.

If there is substantial wealth on both sides – or if one partner brings large assets such as the proceeds of a property sale to the relationship – then it could be worth consulting a lawyer over setting up some form of trust fund. Each of these will be tailormade to suit individual circumstances and needs.

Marriage has a special place in English law even if it has less of a place now in the culture. It can present legal obligations – spouses can find themselves responsible for the debts of wives or husbands, there can be financial settlements on divorce especially if there are children involved – and pension funds can be divided up when a marriage breaks down.

The tax advantages of getting married are minimal compared to what they once were. During the 1990s, the world moved on from a situation where a wife was effectively the tax chattel of the husband to independent taxation and the final abolition – for all other than a dwindling band of those in their late sixties or older – of any tax relief for married couples. This has been replaced by children's tax credit which is targeted at couples – whether married or not – with children where the income of the higher earner is less than around £40,000.

Couples of whatever complexion each have their own tax allowances for Individual Savings Accounts, National Savings, and for capital gains tax, a tax on any profits you make by selling shares and other assets. But married couples have one capital gains tax advantage – they can freely transfer assets between themselves to minimise the tax. Suppose you face a £10,000 capital gains profit. The first £7,500 would be covered by your own allowance. You could then transfer enough of the assets so that the balance of the gain is covered by the spouse's allowance. In this case, this could save up to £1,000. Married couples also have one income tax plus-point, although this is not always applicable.

Income from savings and other investments such as interest and dividends is taxed. But if one partner pays tax at a lower rate than the other, or pays no tax at all, it makes sense to transfer investments into their name so they can maximise the use of the lower or zero level. For instance, if one partner pays top rate tax at 40 per cent, they would lose £400 out of a £1,000 interest payment. But by switching the savings producing this income to a partner who pays no tax, the Inland Revenue can take nothing. There is a drawback in this, however. The transfer has to be permanent. If the relationship breaks down, the money would legally belong to the partner with the lower tax rate.

Many heterosexual couples and a minority of gay relationships look towards parenthood. This may be emotionally satisfying but it is expensive – something that few prospective parents appreciate.

Insurance company claims that it can cost £500,000 or more to bring up a child from the mother's pregnancy to school leaving age can be taken with a pinch of salt. Inevitably, these figures add in factors that few bother with such as nannies and private education. But there is a measure of truth in some of these high figures if one partner stops work to devote themselves to full or part-time childcare. Other less obvious costs include paying more for holidays because they will have to be taken in peak season due to school terms, and having to buy a larger home.

Those who plan for parenthood can try to build up funds to cope with these costs. In most cases, this window of potential money gathering opportunity will only last a few years so cash should probably be directed to savings accounts rather than riskier investments. Some banks and building societies offer better rates for regular savers who agree to put the same amount away each month for a set period.

This time can also be used for building up a pension if one partner intends becoming a full or part-time child carer. The section on pensions has more details but as you cannot save the same amount from limited resources twice, some will have to choose between saving up for a family and buying a pension. In most cases, they will opt for the former – having savings to hand can help buy all the many requisites of child raising. A better pension may be a comfort for the long term, but it will not help with paying for disposable nappies, nursery furniture or the local pre-school group.

Starting a family

Working women have certain financial and workplace rights during pregnancy and the period after the birth. These include:

- Whether the expectant mother works full or part time, she is entitled to reasonable paid time off work for ante-natal care, including relaxation and parentcraft classes as well as medical examinations
- It is illegal to dismiss a woman or select her for redundancy purely or mainly because she is pregnant or has recently given birth.
- Pregnant women are entitled to statutory maternity leave regardless of length of service or hours of work.
- Benefits such as holiday rights or pension fund membership cannot be withdrawn.
- Mothers to be are not automatically paid but could qualify for statutory maternity pay.
- Most employees are entitled to an additional period of maternity absence on top of maternity leave.

Rules for many benefits can be complicated. Local citizens advice bureaux, the Child Poverty Action Group, the Benefits Agency and employers will provide details. Women who wish to claim any maternity rights must tell their employer of their pregnancy and the date the baby is due. This should be backed up by a medical certificate. Bosses are also entitled to three weeks' notice of maternity leave, and three weeks' notice of their date of return if they decide to take an extended period of maternity absence as well as maternity leave.

Whether it is worth combining work with motherhood should be an individual choice based on personal preferences. In many cases, it will be an economic necessity. But more and more women do return to work after having a baby either to fulfil career ambitions such as promotion or to add to the family spending possibilities. If there is any choice in the matter, then it is worth carrying out a basic cost/benefit analysis to help work out the financial consequences.

The obvious benefit is the extra income, which can also include extra pension contributions. Against that, the costs include getting to work, buying smarter clothes, eating out, and, most of all, paid-for childcare. Few UK employers offer crèches and childcare costs can only be set off against tax in a small minority of cases. These are centred on employer-sponsored facilities when the employer provides a crèche as a 'non-cash' benefit and where the employer has a management role in the provision of the childcare. Cash or vouchers that let mothers choose their own childcare are taxable.

Childcare costs up to a weekly limit can be ignored when certain means-tested benefits aimed at the lower paid in work are calculated.

Family benefits

There are a number of state benefits aimed at those with children.

Child Benefit is paid to all – to the mother if she is alive – irrespective of income. It is not taxable. It is currently paid up to school leaving age – to 18 plus for those staying in full time education or an approved form of training. In the 2001–2002 tax year it is paid at £15.50 a week for the eldest or only child, £10.35 a week for other children. There is a lone parent rate of £17.55 for the oldest child in one parent families.

Children's Tax Credit is worth £10 a week to families with children under 16. It is a fixed level benefit paid through the tax system, irrespective of the number of children. Most families can apply but they have to claim – there is no automatic payment. The credit is paid in full where the higher earning parent does not pay top rate tax. Thereafter, the credit is reduced so if the better paid parent earns more than around £42,000, there is no payment.

Working Families Tax Credit is a means-tested benefit aimed at boosting the take-home pay of lower paid households with children. It is complicated and only available to those with less than £8,000 in savings. It can go to employees, who receive the benefit in pay packets, and to the self-employed where payment is made directly. Couples can choose which partner receives the money.

Childcare Tax Credit is associated with Working Families Tax Credit. It covers up to 70 per cent of childcare costs for lower income working parents.

Paying for education

Around one in twelve families pays for private education – anywhere from Eton or Roedean to a local prep school. Look before you take this financial leap – day schools cost from £3,000 to £12,000 a year, while boarding can take the bills up to an annual £18,000 or more. Secondary schools cost more than prep establishments for younger children, but over the 14 years of a typical school career, budget for £150,000 – more if inflation worries you.

If you can afford this level of expense out of your regular income, you probably have no need for advice. But if you cannot, possibilities include:

- saving ahead of the child's need for school fees;
- asking grandparents to help – if they have enough money, it could be better to spend it while they are alive rather than leave to grandchildren in a will when it could face inheritance tax;

- taking out a loan or raising money from the family home via a remortgaging deal;
- taking on extra paid work – some parents have worked night shifts in burger bars to put their children through private education;
- cutting down on luxuries such as holidays, evenings out and cars;
- moving to a cheaper home.

Bear in mind that there are no magic solutions to school fees whatever some so-called 'school fees financial planners' pretend.

One other possibility for those not ideologically wedded to the paid-for school system is simply to find a property in the catchment area of a good state school. The property may be more expensive but not by nearly as much as the cost of funding a private education.

However, whether state or privately educated, parents cannot avoid paying for the one in three who now go to university. Compulsory fees in England and Wales are currently running at around £1,100 a year. Add that to living expenses and it can cost around £25,000 to £30,000 between the first week and ultimate graduation. Parents do have more time to save for this eventuality – many undergraduates also take part time jobs as well as running up bank debt and student loans.

Help from the tax system

Students and others can earn nearly £5,000 in a tax year without paying income tax, and that can include any interest they receive from their own savings. If the tax is not automatically credited by the bank or building society, ask for income tax form R85. You can also ask for repayment of tax paid on accounts held by non-taxpayers for up to the past six years – the local Inland Revenue office will provide a claims form.

But there are limits on the amount of money parents can put into savings accounts in a child's name if the interest is to remain tax free. If more than £100 is earned in any one tax year on money that came from either parent, then the entire interest is taxable at the parent's top tax rate, not just the amount over £100. At a 5 per cent annual interest rate, this equates to a maximum balance of £2,000. Each parent has this limit so two parents can give twice as much.

Tax-free investments such as some forms of National Savings including Children's Bonus Bonds, as well as Friendly Society plans, do not count towards this limit. Friendly society policies including 'baby bonds' have a £25 a month maximum, which must be held for at least ten years. They are only worthwhile if held for at least the minimum period.

Grandparents and others can give as much as they like without income tax worries. They can also give lump sums of up to £3,000 a year each and an unlimited amount of £250 gifts outside possible inheritance tax costs.

Breaking up

Around one in three marriages and other long-term relationships break up. The law is not concerned with unmarried couples, unless there is the welfare of children to be considered where issues such as custody and maintenance often involve the Child Support Agency. Otherwise, it is down to the individuals concerned to extricate themselves as best as possible from purchases bought together, joint bank accounts and home loans.

Divorce can involve all the above plus the legal side of unravelling the marriage contract. But, again, unless there are children involved, there should be few immediate problems if both sides approach the matter without too much mutual hatred (not always possible!).

The most serious issues involve children. Where possible, both sides should attempt to come to an agreement on maintenance payments. Whether they were married or not, this can be the subject of a legal agreement. But where an amicable arrangement is not possible or where one or both parents lives on social security benefits such as income support, the Child Support Agency might become involved. If you are receiving the benefits and the child lives with you, you must generally apply to the CSA for a maintenance assessment. The CSA will require the 'absent' parent to pay towards the child's upkeep.

Beyond that, negotiating a fair splitting of savings and other assets can also be extremely stressful – especially as arguing over money can often be an extension of arguing over the factors that caused the break-up.

There are no hard and fast rules – younger divorcing couples might just decide to split everything down the middle and go their own way and minimise legal bills that neither side can afford. Where more considerable assets are involved, it may be necessary to involve lawyers, accountants and even actuaries.

The biggest decision is usually over the family home. You could:

- sell it and divide any proceeds – the most common course when no children are involved.
- postpone the sale of the home until the children are grown up – solicitors often suggest this. But there are practical difficulties, particularly for the party leaving who may not have enough money to find another home.
- decide that the party who stays buys out the other's share immediately. This can work where one partner has substantial resources.
- decide that one partner keeps the house while the other keeps the investments.

All of these present difficulties to all except the well-off. As a simple piece of economics, it is clear that two people in work will find it easier to pay for and maintain a property than one person. Relationship breakdown is one of the two most common reasons for property repossession – the other is long-term unemployment. Couples breaking up often just hand in the keys to the home to the lender. But this is a move that should not be taken without talking to a debt adviser.

Until recently, pension benefits were virtually ignored in divorce. But they represent savings for the future in just the same way as a bank deposit account. The Welfare Reform & Pensions Act 1999 introduced pensions splitting where the retirement pot is seen as an asset to be divided up.

There are a number of possibilities. Some will go for the 'I keep the house, you keep the pension' arrangement. A number will agree to share the eventual proceeds from the pension, although this can be unsatisfactory as it is up to the pension holder to decide when to retire and on what terms – it does not represent a clean break.

The most usual option now is to value the pension and then divide it according to a formula known as a 'cash equivalent transfer value'. This can work well with money purchase pensions (where the ultimate value depends on stock market returns) but less well with 'final salary' occupational pensions (where the payment depends on earnings in the last year and the length of service).

With final salary schemes, a break-up value based on the current cash equivalent can ignore:

- increases in future earnings, which could be higher than growth in investment returns;
- death in service benefits of up to four times salary;
- taxation, which hits younger divorcees more;
- extra benefits beyond the legal minimum.

Pension splitting mainly affects those whose marriage ends in middle age or later.

Widows and widowers can usually claim a continuation of an occupational pension after their spouses die. But non-married partners, whether of the same or opposite sex, may find it more difficult to claim the same benefits.

Most pension schemes have lump sum death benefits for members dying before retirement age. The scheme trustees usually decide who receives this money. Where there is a married partner, the destination of the cash is easy. In the past, many ignored non-married partners, but now most have realised they have substantial discretion.

The simplest course is for the scheme member to complete an 'expression of wish' form naming the partner as the beneficiary. The form should be updated if there is a change of partner. The trustees are not bound by this – they could split the money in any way they want within their wide legal rights but most will respect wishes in such a document.

Survivors' benefits (usually at a reduced rate) are paid to the widow/widower of a company pension holder. They can also be paid to non-married partners. Where the surviving partner was linked by marriage, there should be no problems. The Inland Revenue does not demand any special tests. But where there is no marriage, the Inland Revenue will allow pension payments to continue to be paid only where financial dependence or inter-dependence can be shown. This means that if the partners lived together and shared their financial resources, the pension should be paid. Those with more casual relationships may be excluded.

Many scheme rules have been updated to treat non-married relationships – including gay relationships – as equal after members' representations and protests. Where rules have not been updated, the trustees may still be able to use thei r discretion to make payments.

It is now possible to 'register a partnership' in some countries. Doing this with your pension scheme, even though informally, could prevent problems and ease matters at an obvious time of strain and stress.

If you have a personal pension, you should contact your insurance company to check that death-before-retirement proceeds go to the person you want to benefit. On retirement, you will need to check that any death benefits from the annuity go where you intend. Whether any such benefits are paid will depend on the terms of the annuity.

6
Retirement

The need for planning

Just why should anyone plan for retirement? It could be 20, 30, 40 or even more years away, and there are always seemingly more urgent needs for your time and money – buying a home, raising and paying for a family, moving up the employment ladder, running a car, or just having a good time. Even when people do think about retirement, it is easy to put decisions off until tomorrow – or the day after that.

The answer to the question is simple, if crude. If you don't bother with planning for your retirement years, then it's unlikely anyone else will. Financially, you may well be on your own.

You will be left to the mercies of the State – currently the basic State pension for a single person is – in rough terms – just £10 day.

There is, of course, no way of knowing what will happen to state pensions in the time to your retirement. They could become more generous – or meaner. No one has any idea. Over the past three or four decades, pension provision from both state and other sources has changed direction several times.

If you do nothing other than rely on state provision, but can afford to do more, you are taking a chance. You may win. You may not. But over those past 30 to 40 years, one thing is certain. Those who built up pensions as a result of their own savings or through a company plan or both have been generally rewarded with a better lifestyle once they gave up the nine-to-five than those that swept the problem under the carpet and ignored their years after work.

Take charge . . .

when you take charge of your own investments you'll make sure others don't just take charges!

When you're looking to invest in stocks and shares, you've a wide range of choices, but one of the first things you need to determine is who's going to make decisions about your investments ... you or someone else.

Naturally, if you want someone to run things for you, through a pension plan, unit trust or managed portfolio for instance, they'll charge you for doing it ... and that's only fair. What you pay will vary from one provider to the next.

But with The Share Centre as the home for your investments you stay in charge, choosing the specific investments that meet your own, personal investment objectives ... so your money works harder for you.

Naturally, you can rely on us to provide all the administration, support and back-up you need ... from efficient low-cost share dealing by telephone, internet or post, to annual tax-return summaries to make your life easier and informed, independent, impartial advice that will help you choose the right shares, decide when's best to buy or sell and provide a friendly ear for when you want another view on your own investment ideas   ... we're always there to guide you.

With all your investments together under one roof it's easier for you to keep control, but it certainly doesn't mean you're spoilt for choice ... you choose how best to hold your investments to ensure you're taking advantage of tax-effective schemes, by using an ISA for instance.

So don't settle for others taking charges ... let The Share Centre put you in charge instead.

Find out how we can help you make the most of your investments ... visit **www.share.com** or call us free on **0800 800 008**

The
Share Centre
Helping you make the most of your investments

Retirement planning is complicated. There are plenty of different types of pension – and there are ways of financing retirement outside of pensions. Every individual will have their own personal mix – and their own aspirations. But there are a number of factors that unite all methods of retirement planning:

- What you have is what you hold. Barring fraud and total incompetence – both have occurred to minorities of pension purchasers over the past decade – money you or your employer puts into a scheme remains yours.
- The more you put in, the more you will get out. A pension is an investment with only one magic extra ingredient – tax relief.
- The sooner you start, the greater the retirement sum you will end up with. A £1,000 lump sum invested at 7 per cent will roughly double in 10 years but only produce about £1,840 after nine years.
- Retiring later works. You will have saved more and have fewer years during which your pension will have to pay you an income.

Back in the 1950s, there was a long running pensions advert from an insurance company. It featured five age viewpoints on pensions. The first was a 25 year-old man – it was all men in those days. He was very happy-go-lucky. As he aged – 35, 45, 55 – his features became glummer and more lined until he was virtually tearing his hair out in desperation when he reached 65. Its thrust is still relevant.

Where to start

Throwing money indiscriminately at a pension scheme may be better than doing nothing – but not much. You could end up locked into an unsuitable plan, which does not provide value for money.

While you need to build up as big an eventual pension pot as you can, planning involves fitting this in with other facets of your financial life. Planning – and seeking advice where necessary – is vital. There are more retirement options, pension providers and investment plans than ever before. You could put the same amount of cash into one plan and end up with substantially more than if you had invested the same money into another. Positive planning can help you avoid poor value schemes and concentrate on those best suited to your needs. These requirements will vary according to your age and circumstances.

Whatever option you end up with, you have to ensure that it is flexible enough to cope both with your changing personal needs – marriage, divorce, job moves, self-employment.

It is all too easy to end up in an unsuitable scheme. You might, for instance, decide to forego a very generous employer plan because a personal pensions poster on the high street caught your eye. While advisers should not suggest this – according to regulators – there is nothing to stop you doing this on your own accord or running into a rogue financial adviser chasing commissions who hopes to have made some money and run away before the mis-selling catches up.

Also, because cash going into a pension plan has largely to be turned into a regular income of one sort or another for the rest of the planholder's life, there are cases of people with terminal illnesses putting money into pensions that they will never be able to draw upon. Again, no adviser should put this forward as an idea but there is nothing to prevent individuals from putting themselves in this inappropriate situation.

You can organise your own pension if you do not have a company plan. Or you can buy one from a company that offers no more than a narrow choice. But unless you are very confident and well versed, independent financial advice may be no more expensive.

Pension buyers have to be realistic. Retirement plans start off with an initial boost from tax relief but then depend on a mix of charges and investment performance for their progress. Charges are lower than they used to be, but so too are investment returns.

The flip side of today's less dramatic gains is lower inflation. If your money has grown 5 per cent a year and prices rise by 2 per cent, you have a real 3 per cent advance. But money growing at 10 per cent a year, when prices are increasing by 10 per cent, only leaves you where you were in purchasing power terms.

LIFE STYLE
FINANCIAL SERVICES
Taking care of tomorrow

- **Ethical Investments**
- **Pensions**
- **On-line Financial Planning**
- **Life Assurance**

www.moneywells.co.uk

FREEPHONE 0800 1380851

Lifestyle Financial Services, Socially Responsible Investment Centre,
Fourteen Wright Street, Kingston upon Hull, HU2 8HU.

Member of the Ethical Investment Research Service. Member of the UK Social Investment Forum.
Registered in England No. 2254373. Mortgage Code Registration 4652310.

Regulated by the FSA for Investment Products.

Pensions planning involves:

- considering how long you wish to continue working – the longer you work, the more a pension fund will grow and the fewer years your fund will have to keep you. Early retirement is expensive retirement.
- thinking about your age – while the earlier the better is a good rule, there is much that can be achieved with 'catching up' – this chapter offers tips to late starters.
- your income – this determines to a large extent how much can be invested in your retirement planning. Don't forget other needs such as insurance, mortgages, savings, and daily living expenses.
- dependants – both how you finance pension contributions and the scheme you choose may depend on whether you have a family to take care of or not.
- what you have already – many will have built up pensions either at work or through private plans. Many of these will be schemes to which you may no longer contribute. Fitting these into your future planning is as vital as selecting a way forward.
- your employment status – those who are self employed, on short term contract work, or not working may need different strategies to those who are in long term jobs.
- your aspirations – as you age, you get a better idea of how much you will need as a retirement income.
- State provision – this may not be generous but it cannot be ignored, especially for those on low incomes.

The pensions puzzle

The world of pensions is an alphabet soup of initials and a maze of schemes.

State schemes

Everyone working in the UK – whether employed or self-employed – should be covered by the basic state pension. Payments depend on an individual's national insurance contribution (NIC) record so those with periods of living abroad may find they have gaps. Claimants of certain state benefits are also covered as they can have contributions credited.

You may also be in SERPs – the State Earnings Related Pension Scheme – which started in 1978. Although benefits have been reduced compared to the original promise, this still offers a pension based on earnings (within annual lower and upper limits roughly equivalent to minimum earnings for national insurance purposes up to one and a half time average national wages) and inflation-linked increases.

SERPs only applies to those in employment. It is obligatory unless the employer offers a substitute scheme that is at least as good – this is called 'contracting out'. If there is no suitable workplace scheme, individuals can also opt out of SERPs providing part of their national insurance payments are used to fund a personal pension. This national insurance rebate varies according to age and sex.

The government is also shortly planning to introduce a 'state second pension (S2P)' aimed at helping the lower paid.

Separately, older people may have entitlement to a claim under the State Graduated Pension, which ended in 1978.

Non-State schemes

All other pension plans are financed either by an employer or by the pension holder or both. They qualify for tax relief up to the pensions earnings limit – £95,400 in 2001/2002. A basic 22 per cent rate taxpayer can buy £100 of payments for £78; someone on the top 40 per cent rate pays £60.

Stakeholder pension purchasers are effectively treated as basic rate taxpayers even if they do not pay tax or only pay at the 10 per cent level.

Pension fund investment managers can reclaim tax on interest paid on bonds or bank deposits, on income from property, and do not pay capital gains tax. But apart from a tax-free lump sum payable at retirement, eventual payments out of pension schemes are taxed.

Climb on early and watch your investment grow

Alliance Select Pension for Children

Create a solid foundation for your child's financial security.

Invest in an Alliance Select Pension for your child and contribute up to £3,600 gross in any tax year[†]

Choose a core, long term investment in the Alliance Trusts* providing diversified global growth investment. Then build your child's pension portfolio choosing from over 200 investment trusts, 400 UK equities plus gilts and corporate bonds.

No annual charges - just transaction based charges - so you control the costs.

Call 01382 306006 or complete the coupon below for details.

Visit us at www.alliancetrusts.com

Alliance Trust Savings Limited

[†] *Assuming basic rate tax at 22% that means a cash contribution of £2,808 and £792 tax relief which we claim and add to your pension, even if you are a non-tax payer.*

* *The Alliance Trust PLC and/or The Second Alliance Trust PLC*

Products are provided on a direct offer transaction basis and administered by Alliance Trust Savings Limited, PO Box 164, Meadow House, 64 Reform Street, Dundee, DD1 9YP (ATS). ATS is an authorised institution under the Banking Act 1987 and is regulated by the Personal Investment Authority for investment business. Charges are transaction based and may be high or low depending on how you manage your investments.

The value of investments and any income from them may fall as well as rise. Once contributed cash may not be withdrawn except for the purposes of pension benefits after the age of 50. Past performance is not necessarily a guide to future performance.

ATS does not give advice. If you have any doubts whether this product is suitable for you, you should obtain independent advice. For security and compliance monitoring purposes telephone calls may be recorded.

Please send me details of the **Alliance Select Pension for Children.**

Name ....

Address ....

.... Postcode ....

☐ I would also appreciate a leaflet on the Alliance Select range of products.

Alliance Trust Savings Limited, PO Box 164, Meadow House, 64 Reform Street, Dundee DD1 9YP.

DE/SUMMER/01

Occupational pensions

Most bigger firms and organisations offer employees pensions, although the rules and benefits may depend on status – boardroom pensions are often better than those paid to shopfloor workers. Companies employing five or more must make a 'stakeholder' pension plan available but there is no obligation on employers to make any contribution.

There are two main types of occupational scheme:

- *Final salary* (or 'defined benefit') promises to pay a pension based on your earnings in your last year at work (there are special rules to take care of those with sharply fluctuating incomes) adjusted for the number of years spent in that scheme. A typical plan might offer one eightieth of final salary for each year so someone earning £40,000 after 20 years would have 20/80 (or 25 per cent) of their final salary as a pension – £10,000 a year. Pensions are also normally increased annually once in payment.
- *Money purchase* (or 'defined contribution') is where an employer invests a pre-set percentage of your salary into a plan so higher earners enjoy greater contributions. But there is no promise of final pension payments. What you end up with depends on a mix of contribution levels, investment performance, costs, and 'annuity' rates.

Both final salary and money purchase plans allow holders the alternative of a reduced pension and a tax-free lump sum. Most go for this option.

Defined benefit schemes present an open-ended cheque to companies so many are abandoning these plans – at least for new employees – in favour of the certainty and lower costs of defined contribution plans.

The majority of occupational schemes of both types are 'contributory' – they deduct a percentage (usually around 6 per cent) from employee salary payments. A minority are 'non-contributory'.

Companies also offer AVCs – Additional Voluntary Contributions or 'top-up' pensions. You can pay up to 15 per cent of salary less any contributory payments already made. These grow in the same way as money purchase plans but tax-free lump sums were phased out in 1988. Some employers offer incentives for AVCs, matching each pound you contribute with between 25p to £1 of their own.

Insurance companies sell FSAVCs – Free Standing Additional Voluntary Contributions plans. These have similar rules to AVCs except they are not tied to an employer. They have the advantage of choice. And they are also portable so they can follow you from job to job. But they are expensive and may not be the best way forward. Employers are unlikely to pay into an FSAVC and there have been FSAVC mis-selling scandals.

Stakeholder pensions are likely to be a better option than AVCs or FSAVCs for qualifying employees.

Personal pensions

These are money purchase schemes bought by individuals. They have been available since 1988, although comparable schemes have been on offer since the 1950s.

Personal pensions appeal to those outside occupational plans including the self-employed and those on short-term contracts. Contributions are invested in a variety of plans but most are 'with-profits' or 'managed' – both labelled as lower risk schemes. These buy into a mix of shares, bonds and property.

You can invest either lump sums or regular payments – provided premiums are within the maximum percentage of your earnings for your age group. You can cash in your pension at any time from 50 to 75.

Up to 25 per cent of the final pension pot can be taken as a tax-free lump sum. The balance has to be used to buy an annuity before you pass 75. An annuity is a promise from a life company to pay a regular amount each month or year in return for the 'pension pot' until you die. After that, the annuity is normally worthless – although your partner may be entitled to some ongoing benefits. With basic annuities, there is no return of your cash even if you fail to collect even one payment.

Stakeholder pensions

The new 'stakeholder' pensions, introduced in April 2001, are a variation on the personal pension formula. They are like personal pensions because:

- they appeal to the self-employed and those without a good workplace scheme;
- their value grows in line with underlying scheme investments;
- there is a tax free lump sum facility;
- holders must eventually buy an annuity;
- higher-rate taxpayers can claim higher tax relief.

But there are significant differences.

- The government has imposed a 1 per cent annual charges ceiling to prevent mis-selling. Some sellers may, however, charge a fee for their advice.
- Investments start at £20 – you are free to add to this whenever you wish but you need not. Some schemes may have a lower minimum.
- There are no penalties for missed or reduced payments or for transferring the pension to another provider.
- Non-earners – whether they are women on career breaks, carers or children – can save for a pension and for the first time get back basic rate tax relief.

Other pension plans include:

- *Retirement annuity plans* – a form of personal pension sold before April 1988. Annual maximum contributions are lower but the tax-free lump sum can be higher.
- *Executive pension plans* – occupational schemes aimed at the management suite and boardroom. These can accelerate benefits.
- *SIPPs* – self-invested personal pensions – a form of personal pension where holders (or their advisers) select investments instead of insurance company fund managers.

ETON SQUARE FINANCIAL MANAGEMENT

The introduction of stakeholder pensions has made it clear that, whatever political party is in power for the rest of our working lives, we'll have to take on a lot more responsibility for our own futures. The welfare state may not yet be dead and buried, but we can no longer rely on the Government even to pretend to be paying pensioners enough to live on. Instead, Gordon Brown has designed a pension product which is meant to be cheap, efficient and easy to understand.

If that's the case, why should you consult a financial adviser before choosing your stakeholder pension? According to Alec Shapiro, Managing Partner at Eton Square Financial Management, you shouldn't – not if that's really all you want to know.

"Stakeholder was introduced to help lower- paid people," explains Alec, "so the structure is deliberately very simple. What's particularly important to the consumer is that the transfer value is always the same as the actual fund value – unlike traditional pension schemes – so you can transfer from one scheme to another without losing anything. But to be frank, with overall charges limited to 1% of contributions, a financial adviser isn't going to be making enough from recommending one to cover the cost of the meeting and all the paperwork that goes with it."

For higher earners though, it's a different story.

FIRST, you can take out a stakeholder pension for every member of the family – including children – investing up to £3,600 for each person, tax free, every year. So if you have spare cash after using up your ISA allowance it's ideal.

SECOND, you can include an income protection scheme and life assurance within the stakeholder pension, again tax free.

THIRD, if you opt for a "stakeholder friendly" scheme (where charges are capped at 1.5% rather than 1%) you'll find a wider range of funds to choose from.

"At Eton Square, we like to treat stakeholder pensions as just one of the products our clients should be thinking about," Alec continues. "As an independent firm – and despite, or even because of our lengthy experience in the tied sector – we like to work with our clients on their long-term financial planning, aiming to create wealth and ensure long term security. Typically, we'll meet three or four times a year – not to sell them another product but to make sure that they're happy and that things are going according to plan. As we rely on recommendations for most of our new business, this means we have to give good advice that pays off in the medium and long term."

And it's not just individuals who should be thinking about stakeholder pensions. Companies with five or more employees have to provide schemes for their employees, though it's not compulsory for staff to join their employer's scheme.

Alec again "We'd advise company directors to look at the big picture and see how stakeholder works within the package that they offer their staff. There's a legal obligation to set up a scheme, so it makes sense to do it so that everyone benefits."

ETON SQUARE
Independent Financial Advisers

Creating Sharper Solutions

for

Corporate & Personal

■ Wealth Creation ■

■ Investments ■

■ Pensions ■

Telephone: 020 7431 4233

Facsimile: 020 7431 4033

11 McCrone Mews, Hampstead London NW3 5BG

NO FUNDING FOR OUR FUTURE

In the UK, around 40% of all social security spending goes on state pensions. This spending does not come out of an underlying fund ñ it is paid for out of taxes on today's working population. Today's workers pay for today's pensioners. The question is – will tomorrow's workers be able to support you in your retirement?

Our life expectancy is ever improving: in 1900 the average life expectancy at birth for a woman was 49, today it is 80. At the same time, the number of pensioners has increased by nearly 50%. So, the cost of state pensions will double in the next 50 years, the UK economy will also grow so that the actual cost compared with the country's growth will remain fairly constant. This means that the cost of state pensions will remain under control. So what's the problem?

STATE PENSIONS VALUE DECLINES

The problem is that state pensions will remain affordable because its value will decrease. Because state pensions now increase each year in line with price inflation, and not in line with wages (which tend to increase at a higher rate), state pensions will reduce in real terms. In 1978, the basic state pension was worth around 20% of average male earnings. Currently, it is worth around 15% and by 2040, it is estimated to be worth just 8%.

The current basic state pension for a single person is, at present, £67.50 a week, assuming a full National Insurance contribution record. Many people already consider this to be inadequate – even the Government makes sure that pensioners have more than this by giving them extra money in the form of means tested benefits. However, if the basic state pension in 1948 had been uprated in line with prices only, then today it would be worth just £25 a week.

STAKEHOLDER PENSIONS

To face these challenges, the Government is proposing a number of changes. One of these initiatives is the introduction of stakeholder pension schemes from April this year. These are intended to encourage individuals to increase their private retirement savings by offering them a simple, cheap and flexible pension plan.

Stakeholder pensions have to meet the following ëminimum standards':

A maximum charge of 1% of the fund, and no other charges.

Freedom to pay as little as £20 at any one time.

No restrictions on the way contributions are made (although stakeholder schemes can refuse to accept contributions paid by cash or a credit card).

A default investment strategy, if the individual does not wish to select one or more investment funds themselves.

Free transfers into and out of the plan – if individuals wish to transfer pension funds into a stakeholder, they cannot be prevented from doing so.

Clear information once a year detailing the contributions paid in and the investment growth.

SO WILL OUR EMPLOYERS LOOK AFTER US?

All employers with five or more employees will have to choose a registered stakeholder pension scheme for their employees, unless they already provide a company pension scheme, or contribute to a personal pension scheme. They will have to provide certain information about the chosen stakeholder scheme to their employees and allow representatives of the scheme into the workplace. However, as the legislation stands at present, although employers have to set up a scheme they will not actually have to contribute to the scheme for you.

STAKEHOLDER AVAILABILITY

Stakeholder pension schemes will be available from supermarkets and high street stores, as well as from traditional insurance companies. The Government is developing a series of ëdecision trees' which are designed to provide information about the options available so that people can decide whether to contribute to a stakeholder pension scheme, and how much to contribute, without the need to take financial advice.

It will be possible to pay up to £3,600 a year into a stakeholder pension regardless of how much a person earns – in fact no earnings are needed at all. For the first time, people who are not working will be able to contribute to a pension – this will allow carers, mature students, parents on a child-care break in employment, the unemployed and people (usually women) whose income is from a divorce settlement, to make pension provision for their future. It will also enable husbands (usually) to help their non-earning wives and children.

All contributions by individuals to a stakeholder scheme will qualify for tax relief – this means that basic rate tax will be added by the Inland Revenue to each contribution. Higher rate payers can claim extra tax relief through their tax returns.

It is possible to pay more than £3,600 a year up to an age-related maximum, but then earnings are required. Once these higher-rate contributions start, they may continue at the same rate for five years after earnings stop.

All these changes are designed to encourage people to make their own retirement provision so that they do not have to rely on state benefits which only provide benefits at around the poverty level. Whether stakeholder schemes will achieve this without compelling people to contribute remains to be seen. Despite being simple in many ways, there are still many rules and regulations around stakeholder pensions. If, when the stakeholder schemes are available from April this year, not enough people start to contribute, the Government might decide to bring in compulsory contributions (from both employers and employees/the self-employed).

Chris Bellers
Manager, Pensions research and development
Friends Provident Life office

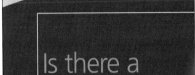

Is there a pension that:

Gives you financial
independence?

Fits with your family's needs?

Copes with career breaks
and temporary employment?

Offers you a low cost and
simple way to save?

Yes...

stakeholder pension solutions
from Friends Provident –
available from 6th April 2001.

Full terms and conditions are
available on request.

Our solution fits with
how you want to live.

- *SSASs* – small, self-administered schemes – a variant of occupational schemes aimed at directors of smaller companies where plan holders (or advisers) select investments.
- *Buy-out bonds* (also known as Section 32 policies) – lump sum investments transferred from a previous employer scheme to an insurer.

Starting out

Understandably, you are unlikely to be very interested in pensions in your twenties – but pensions are an important feature of pay packages. You may find there is a trade-off between present earnings and future retirement income – a 'have it now or have it later' choice.

The best deal is a final salary plan – preferably non-contributory so you pay nothing. You are unlikely to collect your final salary payment from your present employer, but you will be able to leave your pension to grow – or transfer it to another provider if you leave. But good final salary schemes are becoming rarer.

You may instead be offered a money purchase plan. These schemes work best when you have youth on your side. With around 30 to 40 years to go before retirement, you should catch some investment upwaves. And if you change jobs, money purchase plans can be more portable. If you leave a job with a pension plan within two years, you can apply for a refund of your contributions. But you will have to repay tax relief and forego the employer's payments.

Whatever work offers you, if basically you earn less than £30,000 you can still put up to £3,600 a year into a stakeholder plan – £2,808 in cash after basic rate tax relief. This does not have to be from your own money – a parent or grandparent can help with the premiums. Time is on your side, although each year's delay is costly.

You could aim for a fund with higher than average risk – investing directly into equities with a fair slice of overseas shares – rather than a safety first plan. Time is the antidote to investment risk.

Twenty-somethings

Barry, 24, has joined a generous company scheme where each year counts as one-sixtieth for the final salary calculation. If he stays 40 years, he will hit the Inland Revenue maximum of two-thirds (40 × 1/60) of his last pay packet.

Andrew is earning an above average £25,000 with a money purchase scheme. He and an employer together would need to pay in around £660 a month before tax relief to fulfil his ambition of quitting when he is 60 on two-thirds salary with a reasonable provision for a widow's pension.

He could not achieve this on his own – the Inland Revenue maximum contribution for this age and earnings level would be £364 a month for a personal or stakeholder pension or £312.50 per month if he paid into an employer scheme. This is calculated at 17.5 per cent of his earnings for a personal or stakeholder and 15 per cent for an employer scheme.

Retiring on 50 per cent at 60 would still break the rules – it would require around £500 a month. As for retirement at 50, forget it. Even if allowed by the Inland Revenue, Andrew would need to pay around £888 a month – around half his salary.

Thirty-somethings

If you are a professional downhill skier, you can retire when you are 30. Models, footballers, tennis players and other sports full-timers have to wait to 35. But for most, retirement is still up to 30 years away.

This is the time of maximum calls on your cash for housing and family expenses. But your salary may be increasing. And once you pass your 36th birthday, you can invest up to 20 per cent of your earnings into a personal or stakeholder pension if you qualify.

One likely problem for those in occupational pensions is what to do when changing jobs. These are the most likely options in most schemes:

- Leave the fund as a 'deferred' (also known as preserved or frozen) pension. You will be able to cash it in when you reach the scheme's retirement age. Your payment will then represent your service and salary on your leaving date, upgraded each year by up to 5 per cent.

- Turn it into a 'buyout plan'. The trustees of your company scheme value your plan and transfer it to a pension plan with an insurance company where it should grow.
- Assign your pension to the scheme operated by your new employer.
- Take a cash value from the trustees and buy a personal pension with the lump sum.

These decisions do not have to be made immediately on changing jobs. You have time to take advice.

Richard has done nothing about pension planning. Now he's 34 and wants to retire at 60 on half his future earnings – over £92,000 if he continues to get 4 per cent annual pay rises on his present £35,000 – with provision for a widows pension too. To achieve this, he would need to be contributing around £1,000 a month now. This is beyond the Inland Revenue contribution limits for his age and earnings so he would have to find a job where the employer is willing to contribute. Alternatively, he could agree to work to 65 to make his pension more affordable.

Angela is also 34 and earns £35,000 with hopes of retiring on half pay at 60. She has transferred a fund worth £20,000 from a previous employer. She would need total contributions of just over £800 a month from her own pocket and that of her employer.

Forty-somethings

In your forties, your earnings may still be rising but costs start to fall as children leave home and mortgages approach maturity. If you work for, or are a director of, a small or medium-sized company that is prepared to be flexible, and your pensions payments have fallen behind, consider 'salary sacrifice'. This enables the firm to finance an executive pension plan (EPP). Here's an example.

Joanna runs her own company. She earns £50,000 a year and pays the maximum 15 per cent (£7,500 a year) into her pension. Her firm matches this. But she is a late comer to pensions and wants to catch up. She cuts her salary by £5,000. Her maximum contribution now falls to £6,750 but her company has saved £5,000 plus national insurance. It can pay an extra £5,950 into her plan.

The drawback is her salary has to be reduced for all purposes – her insurance policy that pays salary-related sick pay and mortgage applications, for example.

This age group does not have the monopoly on divorce. But the longer a marriage lasts and the greater the earnings power of those involved, the bigger the financial settlement. A pension is an asset just like a property. There are now several ways of dividing it on divorce:

- Split the pension in an agreed ratio. The 'non-pension' ex-partner would then take a transfer value and set up a personal scheme.
- Offset the value of the pension against other assets – typically one keeps the pension, the other the home.
- 'Earmarking' part of the benefits for the spouse when the holder retires – the least likely course.

Many people realise at this age that they have done little to sort out a pension – and need to do much.

William is 44, self-employed and wants to start a pension plan. He currently earns £35,000 a year and wants to retire at 60 on half earnings. He cannot – he would need to pay in around £1,800 a month (£21,600 a year) based on current insurance company projections. The Inland Revenue maximum for his age and earnings is £583 a month so the best he could hope for is around a sixth of his present wages. But if he worked to 65, he would get nearly a quarter of present earnings – as well as having more time and opportunity to save elsewhere to fund his retirement years.

Fifty-somethings

Croupiers and newscasters can retire at 50 on a full occupational pension, thanks to special Inland Revenue rules. The rest of us could either be desperate to retire or eager to work for as long as possible.

Whatever option you choose, it is time to find out what your pensions are worth. You may have several – occupational, personal and state. Find out the transfer or cash-in value of old occupational and personal schemes. A pensions adviser or actuary will estimate your potential retirement income, although you will have to pay for this.

If these old plans are substantial, it might be worth transferring them into one personal pension plan. There are costs involved but you will have options that could help maximise the eventual value of your plan.

One is to opt for 'lifestyle' investment. This is a lower risk strategy which progressively moves your pension pot to safer parts of the risk spectrum – from equities to a 'balanced' portfolio to bonds and finally to cash. Schemes vary but most will take around five to ten years over this process.

An alternative is the Self-Invested Personal Pension (SIPP). This gives you – or your adviser – control over the contents of the plan. A SIPP can be useful in 'phased retirement' – where a fund is gradually turned into a pension leaving the balance to grow. This can apply when someone intends carrying on working part time or if they have other sources of income. SIPPs are usually only advisable if you have a £100,000 minimum in a pension plan.

Theresa and Ian own their own company as directors. They have some pension provision but much of their wealth is tied up in the firm. Using a Small Self-Administered Scheme (SSAS) they can, within limits, invest their pension in the shares and premises of their own company. They can also put part of their pension money into mainstream investments including quoted shares and insurance plans. SSAS rules are complicated so they have to use a recognised scheme provider.

People who have left it too late to start their pension planning have a lot of catching up to do. A 54-year-old man earning £55,000 hoping to retire at 65 on half his present salary would have to pay around £3,750 a month into a pension plan. This is impossible – it is nearly three times the Inland Revenue personal pension maximum for this age of 30 per cent of earnings. And it would cost more than he could possibly afford. So the best he could hope for is to retire on around one-sixth of present earnings – around £9,000 a year.

However, if he was willing to work until he reached 75, he could pay around £1,300 a month – a sum within the Inland Revenue limits – and retire on half pay. He should check on the policy to ensure that it repaid the fund in full were he to die over the next 20 years.

Sixty-somethings

Men can draw their state pension at 65; women born before April 1950 at 60; those born after March 1955 at 65 (there is a sliding scale between these two dates). You can defer drawing the state pension for up to five years. This increases the eventual payment.

Final salary company schemes should start as soon as you retire – there are special rules to help if your earnings were low in your last year, perhaps through illness.

Personal pensions are generally cashed in through annuities. Annuities are life insurance policies in reverse. Instead of paying in each month and receiving a lump sum on death, holders pay a lump sum and receive a regular income until they die. You do not have to buy the annuity from your pension provider. The 'open market option' offers the freedom to shop around.

Annuity rates are based on how long the life company thinks you will live – men tend to die before women so males get higher rates – and on interest rates on long-term government bonds.

There are a variety of annuities including:

- joint life annuities, which pay until the second person dies.
- guaranteed annuities, which pay for a fixed period even if the holder dies.
- escalating annuities, which increase payments each year – either a fixed percentage or by the rate of inflation.
- with-profits annuities – these invest your fund in a mix of equities and bonds with the goal of producing an eventually higher rate.
- impaired life annuities – these pay more to heavy smokers or to those with serious illnesses.

Stuart, 62, is in the fortunate position of not needing all his pension now. He still has earnings from work and he would lose 40 per cent of his payments to higher rate tax. He puts all his pensions into a personal plan, which is then divided into segments or 'mini-policies'. He phases turning the segments into annuities over 10 years to fit in with his overall financial planning.

He swaps the certainty of an annuity now for the flexibility of phased retirement. He is willing to take investment market risks. He has to convert the entire plan into an annuity by 75. But if he dies before, the value of remaining segments goes to his family.

Even in your sixties you can still catch up. At this age, you can put up to 40 per cent of your income into a personal pension; if you are in an occupational scheme, you could still invest up to £3,600 a year into a stakeholder plan providing you earn less than £30,000 a year and are not a director.

You can take advantage of tax relief on contributions and the tax-free lump sum to almost get something for nothing – especially if you are a higher rate taxpayer.

Pauline is a 40 per cent taxpayer. She pays in a £10,000 lump sum – £6,000 in cash with the balance from tax relief. She retires the next day. She collects a tax free lump sum of £2,500 (25 per cent) leaving £7,500 to buy an annuity which has effectively cost £3,500 (£6,000 in cash less the £2,500 lump sum.

This tactic also produces benefits, although lower, for basic rate taxpayers. *(NB this example ignores costs.)*

Alternatives to pensions

Pensions are just one way to save for retirement. Other methods include:

● *Individual Savings Accounts.* There is no tax relief on contributions but investments grow free of tax while dividends and interest are paid out tax-free. You can invest up to £7,000 each tax year.

● *Buy-to-let.* Buying properties to rent out. Special mortgages are available. The idea is the rental income pays off the mortgage by retirement – leaving a continuing pension income stream as well as a valuable property.

● *With-profits and other insurance bonds.* These can offer a regular income from a lump sum investment with some tax advantages for higher rate taxpayers.

● *Zero dividend preference shares.* These come from split-capital investment trusts. They can be used to provide tax favoured lower risk income payments.

Return Used LaserJet Cartridges to hp and give them a Second Chance

Have you ever wondered what happens to your company's old LaserJet print cartridges? Laser printers are used on a huge scale nowadays by large and small businesses alike with many used print cartridges eventually ending up in landfill sites.

But if your company is part of Hewlett-Packard's LaserJet Print Cartridge Return and Recycling Programme, you can be reassured that your cartridges will be disposed of far more efficiently and without damage to the environment.

Last year in the UK alone over 320,000 cartridges were returned to hp, where their parts were converted into a raw material used to make thousands of everyday objects like buttons, bins or bicycle stands. Since the programme started in 1996, hp has recycled over 31 million LaserJet cartridges globally.

So thanks to our customers, more than 40 thousand tonnes of waste – that's the weight of 500 Boeing 747 planes – have been diverted away from landfill sites around the world.

Refill or Recycle?

Some consumers may choose to refill or buy refilled toner cartridges, believing that they are acting environmentally. In reality they are just prolonging the moment when the cartridge will be discarded into a landfill site – refilling is not an environmentally viable alternative to recycling your old print cartridges.

In addition, refilling toner cartridges by hand is a potentially dangerous activity as toner is made up of extremely fine particles which can be unsafe if accidentally inhaled. And refilling provides no financial advantage to your company. In fact it may even reduce the life and performance of your print cartridge making print quality less reliable over time.

Free to all its customers, hp's LaserJet Print Cartridge Return and Recycling Programme provides a much safer and more convenient alternative to customer refilling. And it guarantees that your old LaserJet print cartridges will be genuinely recycled which reduces the amount of waste materials that are thrown away.

How To Take Part

HP LaserJet cartridges can only be recycled if socially responsible companies continue to send them back to hp. If you only use a few cartridges a year, simply seal the old cartridges in the packaging that comes with the new cartridge and attach the pre-paid delivery label enclosed in the new box. The box will be returned free of charge to hp.

If your company accumulates a large number of cartridges, call 08456 014751 to request a bulk container. When you have 20 or more cartridges, a local agent will collect them from a designated point.

For more information on hp's LaserJet Print Cartridge Return and Recycling Programme call the customer enquiry centre on 08456 014751.

invent

7

Inheriting It, Leaving It

At some stage in your life, you may inherit money. At a later stage, you may have money and other assets that you wish to leave to others after your death.

Inheriting is easy – all you have to do is decide whether to spend it or invest it. There are no tax charges on money that is left to you once you have it. But the amount you inherit – and the sums you might eventually leave to others – can be affected by taxation between the will and your receipt of the assets. A family could lose up to 40 per cent of the value of what is left in a will. This can be cut – or got rid of completely – with planning.

Making a will

The first stage involves making a will. This can be written by any person aged 18 or over in England and Wales (12 for girls and 14 for boys in Scotland). A will is essential for anyone, no matter what age, with any assets to leave or who might have assets to bequeath in the future. No one knows when they will die. A will is the only way a person can direct what will happen to their wealth after they are no longer around to influence matters.

English law (Scottish law can be different in this area) does not recognise heterosexual partnerships outside of marriage, let alone gay households. And even the right of a married person to inherit the estate of their former spouse is limited if that person dies 'intestate' – without a will. If you want a partner to inherit anything, or a spouse to inherit more than the minimum, a will is essential. You can be in a non-married relationship for decades, produce children together, and still have no legal standing when your partner dies.

'Will' and 'last testament' are synonymous – but they should not be. There is nothing 'last testament' about a will because it can be torn up and replaced at any time.

Wills are automatically made invalid by marriage. Divorce, however, does not end a will, with the exception of specific bequests made to the former husband or wife. Divorce and a subsequent new relationship often complicates matters with step-children and other new family members. It is essential to draw up a new will once a marriage reaches breaking point.

If you know enough about the law, you can draw up your own will on a piece of paper. One step up is to buy a ready made printed will from a stationery shop for about a fiver. For uncomplicated estates where there are few assets and all is being left to one person, this is better than nothing. But what happens if the proposed beneficiary dies before you do? Where do you want your assets to go then?

The easiest solution for most people is to find a professional such as a solicitor or a specialist will-writing firm to help them with their will. This should cost around £50 to £100 with a discount for a second 'mirror-image' will for your partner. A mirror image is where each partner has the same intentions with the only variance being which one dies first. A typical mirror image would have both leaving half the value of their property to the other with the balance divided up among defined children. Property held jointly automatically passes from one partner to the other, irrespective of marital status.

Half of all deaths are without a will, however. In a sizeable proportion of these, the value of what is left is tiny or non-existent. But larger estates could run into the intestacy rules. These are complicated (and different in Scotland). They try to replicate what a typical person might have done had they written a will. There are, of course, no typical persons.

This is how it works. If you have been married for more than 28 days and there are children, your spouse inherits everything up to £125,000 plus personal effects such as clothes, cars, jewellery and other similar items. She/he would then receive the income, but not the capital on half what is left. The other half is shared equally between the children when they reach 18 or when they marry, if earlier. They will inherit the capital half when the income holder dies.

If there are no children, but living parents, sisters, brothers, nieces and nephews then the spouse inherits the first £200,000 plus personal effects plus half of what remains. The rest goes first to parents, if they are dead then to brothers and sisters, and if they do not exist, to nieces and nephews. Only if there is no family will the spouse inherit the rest.

It is even more complicated if you are not married. Partners are not recognised so your entire estate goes through the following family chain:

children (both legitimate and illegitimate but not stepchildren unless adopted)
⇓
grandchildren
⇓
parents
⇓
brothers and sisters and nieces and nephews
⇓
grandparents
⇓
aunts and uncles, cousins
⇓
until it finds a relation who is still living.

If there is no family, the whole estate goes to the Treasury to help pay off the National Debt. This does happen, although the Treasury will often offer to divert the estate to a charity when it can be shown that the deceased person has supported a good cause. It can also use its discretion to help a non-married partner. It is false economy to rely on an estate being worth less than the £125,000 or £200,000 limits (whichever is relevant). Although they are changed from time to time, a sudden increase in a property price or even a national lottery win could take an estate over the limit.

The will writing fee only covers the production of the will. It makes sense to work out who will receive what beforehand. The first essential in a will is to state what form of funeral you want. The costs come out of what you leave.

Debts and taxes also come out of the estate before any beneficiary can profit from bequests. There are three forms of bequest:

- A specific gift such as an item of jewellery or a car to a named person. If the gift ceases to exist or cannot be found, there can be no compensation.
- A pecuniary gift – a fixed sum such as £500. This can be inflation linked. Again, this must go to a named person.
- A residue legacy – whatever is left over to be divided among named persons.

You can leave everything to one person. The will has to be signed by you – and by two witnesses (one in Scotland) who are both present at the same time. Witnesses cannot benefit from a will. They also do not have to read it – all they are doing is affirming that your signature is valid.

You will need to appoint at least two people as 'executors' who will carry out your requests. They can be beneficiaries. Executors can be anyone you trust but it is better to appoint someone such as a younger adult who is likely to outlive you. You can also appoint a bank or a firm of lawyers – there will be fees payable out of your will for this. Banks and many solicitors have a not undeserved reputation for incompetence and high charges.

Wills can be contested, especially if they ignore the needs of dependant spouses or children. Wills can also be rewritten within two years of death if all the beneficiaries affected agree. This is known as a 'deed of variation' or a 'deed of family arrangement'. This can happen when members of a family die in quick succession so the wishes of the original will are no longer appropriate. These deeds can also be used in reducing inheritance tax. But there are ways a will can be used to cut the tax as well.

Inheritance tax

This is the tax that is payable on what is left in your will to those other than a legal spouse after funeral costs and outstanding debts and tax bills. If all the value of your estate – the legal term for everything you leave – goes to your spouse, then there is no tax charge. However on her or his death, the tax will be levied on the full value of what is left. There are no concessions for partners, whether straight or gay. Even property held jointly by a non-spouse can be subject to the tax.

Despite rumours of reform, false alarms about even tougher rules and hopes of abolition, inheritance tax has remained largely unaltered for a decade and more. The Inland Revenue can hold up probate – the legal go-ahead for beneficiaries to be paid – until tax due is agreed. The tax should be paid within six months of the death and the assets cannot be touched (including sold) until the tax is paid.

The tax does not affect most of those who die – but the percentage of payers is growing. The estate has to be worth £242,000 before the tax kicks in (in the 2001/2002 tax year). And then it swallows up 40 per cent of what is left. There is no starter rate. If you leave £300,000, the estate pays 40 per cent on £58,000 (£300,000 less £242,000) or £23,200.

The very wealthy can use a whole host of devices including trusts, insurance plans and offshore planning policies to escape. Those who bear the brunt of the tax are those in the middle. They are neither poor enough nor rich enough to escape.

Financial companies make it sound as though it is easy to escape the tax – they call it a 'voluntary tax' and imply you are stupid if your estate has to pay it. But whether you can plan a reduction or not may depend on your circumstances – on how much you can afford to give away without jeopardising your lifestyle and on how long you live.

Nevertheless, for those who can afford it, there are possibilities. This is how the tax inspector works out the bill. Take the value of *assets* (property; holiday home/caravan; car; bank accounts; stocks and shares; Individual Savings Accounts and Personal Equity Plans – though tax free during life; National Savings; unit trusts; life insurance plans not held in trust; works of art, antiques etc; household contents). From that total, subtract *liabilities* such as all debts, and the funeral, bequests to a spouse and the starter 'nil-rate' band, currently £242,000. What is left is divided 40 per cent to the tax authorities and 60 per cent to beneficiaries.

The objective of planning is to reduce the assets in the estate.

- Ensure all life policies are written in trust. That way they remain outside the estate and can be paid quickly to your family when needed. There is little point in insuring your life for £100,000 and paying premiums on that sum if 40 per cent or £40,000 goes straight to the government. Writing a policy in trust should be straightforward. Life insurers will do it for you.
- Give away as much as you can. Anything you give to others seven or more years before your death escapes the tax. These are called 'lifetime gifts' or potentially exempt transfers. Whatever you give has to be genuinely disposed of. If parents give children the family home, they must either move or pay a commercial rent (which will be taxable in the hands of the home's new owner). Gifts with strings do not count.
- There are also exemptions for small amounts. Everyone can give an unlimited number of gifts of up to £250; there is an additional annual exemption of £3,000 per person; and there are 'wedding gifts' – a maximum of £5,000 for parents of the bride and groom, £2,500 for grandparents and £1,000 for others. These 'wedding gifts' must be made before a marriage and the marriage must be recognised – gay and straight partnerships do not count. These amounts are now fairly modest – they were first established nearly 20 years ago and have never been upgraded since.
- Leave money to charity or to mainstream political parties. These donations are also exempt.
- Make regular gifts out of income. A grandparent could make out a standing order or other regular payment to help with a grandchild's upkeep or education. Provided the gift does not alter the donor's

standard of living and provided that the parents of the child do not then subsidise the grandparent, then it is exempt.

One way that elderly people can both reduce the value of their estate, so cutting the inheritance tax potential, and increase their income in their last years is to turn their home into a source of income.

Home income plans

Home income plans cash in on the value of a property. They appeal to the 'property rich, cash poor' who may have inadequate pensions. House prices have at least doubled for someone now in their late seventies or early eighties who may have retired two decades ago. At the same time, the income they get from their cash deposits in the bank, building society, or National Savings has fallen heavily with interest rate reductions.

In almost all cases, the homeowners are literally that – they have long since paid off their mortgage and collected the deeds to their dwelling.

One solution to square that vicious circle of lower real income and higher real house values is the Home Income Plan which allows owners to unlock the underlying worth of their property while still remaining in their properties. They can then turn this cash into a regular, additional income for the rest of their lives.

In return, the home income plan company will either own all or part of the property – or have a mortgage charge over it which will have to be paid off on the death of the planholder, or both holders in the case of a married couple.

That obviously means that the family will not inherit as much, but this may matter less than the need to have an income boost. In many cases, the 'children' are already into middle age and are comfortably off with property of their own – and around half of all home income plan customers have no direct family to inherit the home.

If home income plans sound a neat idea, that's because to a degree they are, but like so many other solutions to money problems from the financial industry they should be treated with care. Home income plans have been a financial mis-selling zone in the past. More recently, however, there has been new consumer regulation, while the better home income plan providers have set up SHIP – Safe Home Income Plans – to overcome the bad publicity and prove there are secure methods for the elderly to turn the property rich, cash poor equation to their advantage.

SHIP approved schemes guarantee:

- complete security of tenure for the rest of the planholder's life;
- the freedom to move without jeopardising your financial situation – this can be essential if long term care is needed;
- certainty of a secure cash sum or an income for life.

Most home income plans are only suitable for those aged 65 or older. And when a couple apply, most plan providers add up their ages with a total of 135 to 140 being the usual minimum, although some base it solely on the age of the female as she is likely to live longer – a typical female only minimum is 70.

However they are structured, most plans are based on an annuity-type gamble. The plan provider is banking on the elderly person living for a short time, while holders hope to live as long as possible to gain the maximum benefit from their decision.

There are two main types of plan – the reversion and the mortgage-backed loan. A third type, the Shared Appreciation Mortgage proved popular but banks could not finance more than a tiny part of the demand so it may not be currently available.

The reversion involves homeowners signing over all or part of their property to a specialist company in return for a lump sum and the rights to live in the home for the rest of their lives. They must keep the house in good repair at their own cost.

Reversions typically give between 38 and 60 per cent of the property's value in cash with the higher percentages going to older people. A number opt for a partial reversion, swapping a proportion of the property for a smaller cash sum. Reversion companies may give higher amounts if the property owner's life is 'impaired' – anything from suffering from a life threatening illness to having a bad smoking record. When the holders die, the property reverts to the home income plan firm.

Some companies allow the cash to be spent or invested as the plan purchasers want; others insist it is spent on an annuity where a lump sum buys an income for life, however long or short that may be.

Mortgage annuity schemes – or home income loan plans – rely for their success on a fixed interest rate which is less than the value of an income produced by an annuity purchased with the loan.

A typical example for a 75 year old single woman shows that a £30,000 loan produces an annuity of around £3,000. After interest, she has annual extra income of about £1,300 for the rest of her life although this sum may be reduced by income tax on the income portion of the annuity. When she dies, her estate must repay the £30,000 either by selling the property or from other sources.

Factors to look for in these schemes include:

- interest rate – check it is fixed for life as well as being competitive;
- minimum age – there will be one for men, a second for women and a third for couples;
- minimum loan and property value– many companies will not lend less than £25,000;
- advice – some are more helpful than others;
- annuity – are purchasers obliged to buy one and are they free to shop around?
- fees – these vary considerably;
- portability – what happens if the plan holders want or need to move?

Turning part or all of your home into an income can have some unexpected additional advantages. A loan or reversion reduces an estate for inheritance tax purposes. The maths are simple. The owner of a £100,000 home might receive around £40,000 to £45,000 from a reversion. They can then spend or invest the money to produce an income. Had they left it as part of an estate that is large enough to fall into the inheritance tax net, their family would have only received £60,000.

However, for property owners who do not have inheritance tax worries, these schemes are more expensive. On smaller properties, spending your capital while you are still young enough to enjoy it means there is less available to assess for your contribution should you eventually need long term care. So the state will pay for a home sooner. But if your income is low enough to qualify for income support or the Mig guaranteed pension, avoid home income plans. For every £1 you earn from giving up part or all of the value of your home, you will lose £1 from your benefit. You will also run into rules designed to penalise those with more than modest savings.

No one should take out a plan without talking through the implications with their families and with an independent financial adviser. Many schemes insist you discuss the matter with a solicitor before you sign.

Both Age Concern (020 8679 8000 and local branches) and Help the Aged (020 7253 0253 and local branches) have advice leaflets and will provide initial help for anyone considering a home income plan.

Long-term care

Around one in five older people need full-time nursing home care in their last months or years because they are not able to look after themselves (or have no one to do this).

Long-term care is costly – around £350 to £450 a week. In England and Wales, many people will be expected to pay part of these costs from their own resources, which could include selling the family home. In Scotland, moves are under way to make long-term care free.

In England and Wales, the government will pay for the nursing element for everyone but not for personal care and residential costs. This reduces bills by around £100 a week. The State will, however, pick up the entire bill for those with savings below £18,000 with the value of a property excluded for the first three months of the stay. After that, their home is counted.

Insurance companies have seen a sales opportunity in this. They promote 'long-term care policies' which will pay costs if the policyholder needs them and for however long they are necessary. But very few plans have been sold. Despite the insurance company scare tactics, the fact is that only a small percentage of elderly people end up in care for more than a few months. So while the cover provided does apply to a number, it is hard to justify the costs – or for many to pay them in the first place.

Although costs can vary widely, a man aged 55 would have to pay around £50 a month into a typical plan for the rest of his life to produce the minimum likely care home fee of £1,000 a month or pay up a £15,000 lump sum. Women need to find around 20 per cent more.

These costs escalate rapidly as potential planholders get older – a 70 year old woman might need to pay £150 a month to secure possible payments of £1,000 a month.

Funerals

It may not be to everyone's taste but some people are prepared to talk about their eventual demise and funeral expectations. An undertaker is now making coffins in far from standard shapes and colours. Some want to be buried in boxes celebrating their favourite football teams; others have asked for Thomas the Tank Engine style caskets. Charity Age Concern claims that three out of four people over 50 are now 'comfortable discussing their funeral wishes with family members'.

How much does it cost?

Funerals are not cheap – and can become very expensive if someone wants an elaborate send-off.

Gangland funerals in the East End of London may not be everyone's cup of tea. But the estimated £25,000 cost (not counting the police lining the route or the security for other gang members let out of prison for the occasion) of a similar final journey can at least be subsidised by the Inland Revenue.

Funeral expenses come out of a person's estate. Anyone liable for inheritance tax at 40 per cent (those who leave an estate worth more than £242,000) would therefore effectively only pay 60p in each pound.

Undertakers' bills for more traditional funerals vary immensely. Leaving aside extras such as a wake, the average for Scotland – based on a number of surveys – is around £1,600 for a burial and £1,100 for a cremation. Prices for burials tend to be lower in rural areas; highest in city centres due to the pressure on land space. Cremation prices are more uniform.

It is worth asking for competitive quotes, although the Office of Fair Trading says only one in 30 people do this. Prices for burial or cremation in the same place can vary immensely. One survey found that undertakers owned by the giant American SCI group charged around 25 per cent more than independents. One difficulty is that some funeral chains – the Co-op is the biggest competitor – insist on a minimum level such as two cars to follow the hearse whether needed or not. Local funeral directors can be more flexible.

It can be difficult organising and negotiating prices at a time of obvious grief – which is why a degree of pre-planning is helpful.

DIY or green funerals

Burying someone in a cardboard box in a farmer's field is very much a minority interest – but growing. *The New Natural Death Handbook* (published by Rider Books £10.99) lists a number of woodland burial grounds in easy reach of main cities.

The handbook also features suppliers of bio-degradable cardboard coffins, which cost around £50 for those who consider it a waste to bury good timber. But some woodland sites are happy to accept bodies wrapped in just a shroud – which is also a traditional method in many overseas countries and among some faith groups in the UK.

The handbook also explains how to arrange a funeral on a DIY basis – increasingly popular in a secular and multi-faith age. Mourners can use any suitable vehicle for a hearse – big estate cars, builders' white vans and horse and cart have all been used.

Costs are considerably lower than traditional funerals although most woodland style burials have been from choice rather than financial pressure.

The pre-paid funeral

Some 675,000 people a year die in the UK. In total 300,000 people have so far purchased a pre-arranged plan. Age Concern, which has a controversial tie-up with US funeral giant SCI, has sold around 60,000 in three years.

It involves paying out a lump sum in advance, which then guarantees a certain style of funeral whenever death occurs. It is inflation proof and reputable organisations have insurances and trust funds in case the funeral provider goes out of business.

The schemes ensure that the family does not have to worry about the funeral. But the plans can be inflexible. Someone who dies abroad may wish to be buried there. And wishes change – as death approaches someone might want particular religious or other rites.

Expect to pay from £1,200 for a simple funeral up to £2,500 for a grand send-off. Check whether plans include 'disbursements' – cremation fees, doctors' costs and any obituary notices. These can add up to £400.

Insurance

Once upon a time, the door-to-door insurance man would collect an old penny a week the moment a child was born. This would pay out a fixed sum on death whether it occurred one day or 80 years after the policy was started, provided the premiums were maintained. But the £30 or £60 on offer was not inflation proofed.

These policies are no more. They have been replaced by those plans advertised on daytime television and in certain magazines which proclaim 'Aged 50 to 80? Life cover guaranteed without medical tests'. These pay nothing if you die within two years (except in an accident) and a fixed sum thereafter. There is no inflation proofing or other growth.

Typically, those who survive more than seven years would have done better putting their cash into a savings plan – or taking out a prepaid funeral.

The Social Fund

The old concept of the 'pauper's funeral' or getting buried 'by the parish' has gone. Instead, those who cannot afford a funeral for a family member who has died leaving insufficient funds – funerals are always the first claim on an estate – can receive help from the means-tested Social Fund operated by the Department of Social Security.

There are a number of hurdles. Claimants have to receive a means-tested benefit such as Income Support or Housing Benefit. They must show that they are the partner or a close relative of the deceased or they are someone else who would reasonably take care of the arrangements. The Benefits Agency will probe whether there is not another relative with more money who could afford to pay for the funeral.

Payments cover essential burial or cremation costs with an allowance of up to £600 for other expenses such as a hearse or a religious service. Claims – on form SF200 – must be made within three months of the funeral. Local undertakers may be able to offer advice.

The funeral ombudsman scheme

This considers complaints against funeral directors who are members of the Funeral Standards Council scheme. Grounds for claiming compensation include:

- failing to provide services to the standard promised;
- charging more than was agreed;

- carrying out a funeral unprofessionally, inefficiently or with unnecessary delay.

Complaints must firstly be referred to the undertaker within six months – and they must not be the subject of legal action. Details on 029 2038 2046 or website funeral-standards-council.co.uk

Appendix I
Saving and Investing

Accountants

Association of Chartered Certified Accountants
29 Lincoln's Inn Fields
London WC2A 3EE

Institute of Chartered Accountants in England and Wales
PO Box 433
Chartered Accountants Hall
Moorgate Place
London EC2P 23J

Institute of Chartered Accountants of Scotland
27 Queen Street
Edinburgh EH2 1LA

Institute of Chartered Accountants in Ireland
Chartered Accountants House
87–89 Pembroke Rd
Dublin 4

Benjamin, Taylor & Co
5 Wigmore Street
London W1H 0HY
Tel: 020 7636 7176
Fax: 020 7491 2280
E-mail: bt@benjamin-taylor.co.uk

Crompton & Sherling
9 Argyle Street
London W1V 2AT
Fax 020 7734 2761

Ellam & Company
100 New Bond Street
London W1Y 0RE
Tel: 0207 495 0895
E-mail: mail@ellam.demon.co.uk
Web: http: //www.scoot.co.uk/ellam/

H. Rainsbury & Co Chartered Accountants
15 Duncan Terrace
Islington
London N1 8BZ
Tel: 020 7837 4870
Fax: 020 7833 1975

Banks & building societies

Regulators and further information:

Financial Services Authority
25 The North Colonade
Canary Wharf
London E14 5HS
Tel: 0845 606 1234

Financial Services Ombudsman
South Quay Plaza,
183 Marshwall
London, E14 9SR
Tel: 0845 080 1800

Providers:

Abbey National
Abbey House
Baker Street London, WC2B
Tel: 0845 765 4321
Web: www.abbeynational.co.uk

Alliance & Leicester
Web: www.alliance-leicester.co.uk

Allied Irish Bank
Berkeley Square Branch
Berkeley Square, W1X
Tel: 0207 629 8881
Web: www.aib.ie

Barclays Bank
11–12 St. Swithins Lane
London EC4N
Tel: 0207 929 4080
Web: www.barclays.co.uk

Cheltenham & Gloucester
Barnett Way
Gloucester GL4 3RL
Web: www.cheltglos.co.uk

Co-operative Bank PLC,
62/64 Southampton Road,
London WC1B 4AR
Tel: 0345 212212
Web: www.co-operativebank.co.uk

Direct Line Financial Services
250 St. Vincent Street
Glasgow G2 5SH
Tel: Personal Loans: 0208 680 996
Tel: Savings: 0208 667 1121
Tel: Mortgages: 0208 649 9099
Web: www.directline.com

Egg
Web: www.egg.com

First Direct
FREEPOST
Leeds, LS98 2RF
Tel: 0345 100 100
Web: www.firstdirect.co.uk

Halifax plc
Tel: 0845 605 5010
Web: www.halifax.co.uk

HSBC
Personal Financial Services
Poultry
London EC2P 2BX
Tel: 08457 404 404
Web: www.hsbc.com

Lloyds TSB
Tel: 0345 309 072
Web: www.lloydstsb.co.uk

Natwest Bank plc
135 Bishopsgate
EC2M 3UR
Tel: 0207 375 5000
Freephone: 0800 255 200
Web: www.natwest.co.uk

Northern Rock
Northern Rock House
Gosforth
Newcastle upon Tyne
NE3 4PL
Tel: Mortgages: 0845 60 50 500
Tel: Investments: 0845 600 4466
Web: www.northernrock.co.uk

Northern Bank
Web: www.northern-bank.co.uk

Prudential
4th floor, 1 Waterhouse Square
London EC1N
Tel: 0207 548 3541
Web: www.pru.co.uk

Royal Bank of Scotland
1 Fleet Street,
London EC4Y
Tel: 0207 353 4080
Web: www.rbs.co.uk

Standard Life Bank
Standard Life House
30 Lothian Road
Edinburgh, EH1 2DH
Tel: Savings Accounts: 08457 55 56 57
Tel: Mortgages: 0845 845 8450
Web: www.standardlifebank.com

Tesco Personal Finance
Tel: 08457 10 40 10
Web: www.tesco.com/finance

Virgin One account
Discovery House
Whiting Rd
Norwich, NR4 6EJ
Tel: 08456 000 001
Web: www.virgin-direct.co.uk

Woolwich plc
Web: www.woolwich.co.uk

Yorkshire Bank plc
Web: www.ybs.co.uk

Stocks & shares

Regulators and sources of further information:

Association of Private Client Investment Managers
112 Middlesex Street
London E1 7HY
Tel: 020 7247 7080

Association of Investment Trust Companies
Durrant House
8–13 Chiswell Street
London EC1Y 4YY
Tel: 020 7282 5555

Financial Services Ombudsman
South Quay Plaza,
183 Marshwall
London, E14 9SR
Tel: 0845 080 1800

HOW TO CHOOSE AND USE AN ONLINE BROKER

Peter Temple

There is more to choosing a broker than simply selecting the one with the lowest commission rate. Different individuals want different services from their broker and what suits one may not suit everyone.

Those contemplating opening a broking account to deal in shares for the first time can be forgiven for being confused, but there are some basic requirements you can look for, such as: real-time dealing; a reputation for reliability and efficient administration; and easy account-opening procedures.

StockAcademy (www.stockacademy. com), as one example, scores on all these points, but has been particularly commended on the last. The site claims that anyone on an electoral roll, with a debit card and sufficient cash, can open an account in nine minutes.

Another basic but critical factor to consider when selecting an online trading service is how user-friendly the site is. Some sites pack supposedly sophisticated features onto the home page, with the essentials (namely, what stocks you can deal in and what the service costs) lost in a maze of confusing design. Techniques that appeal to designers are often a nightmare for customers, more so in the broking area than anywhere else, because time is potentially money.

When looking for a trading site, bear in mind that most online brokers offering real-time dealing in UK equities are all connecting clients to the automated execution services operated by leading market makers. This aspect of the service ought to be the same whichever service you use. So the real difference in quality comes from elsewhere, such as the level of market information available.

Let's continue with our example. Good brokers often have links on their site to other financial information providers, just as StockAcademy has with UK-invest.com (www.ukinvest.com), the award winning online financial news provider.

The alliance benefits StockAcademy in that clients, or indeed anyone that surfs the site, has access to both general news stories and announcements relating to specific stocks, able to be searched for by inputting a company name or EPIC code (a standard three or four letter acronym used for quick identification of a share).

Corporate web sites are also useful for in-depth research on companies. Most companies worth investing in have them, and the best among them contain detailed financial information, press releases, analyst presentations and other helpful information.

Assuming that your research is complete, it's time to go back to the broker site and start trading. Most sites (and the example of StockAcademy is no exception) work via what might be called an online dealing 'ticket'.

If this is a new concept to you, think of it as a simple form that lets you specify which stock you are interested in, whether you want to buy or sell, the quantities involved and whether or not you wish to place a limit price above which you do not wish to buy or below which you do not wish to sell.

Instead of giving this information to a dealer over the phone, you simply type in the data and, after checking it's correct, hit the appropriate button on the web page to confirm.

Before the order is sent to the market, it's normal for you to enter a PIN number for security reasons. This needs to agree precisely with your login and password for the order to be valid. In the case of a buy order, the system will also check that you have enough credit in your account to pay for the purchase, or in the case of a sale, that the stock is actually one you hold.

Once accepted, the market response is to provide a price that is good for 15 seconds. If you accept the dealing price and hit confirm before the 15 seconds are up, then the deal is transacted instantly and a contact note itemising the deal emailed to you.

However, investors soon become aware (usually after their first few deals have lost money!) that there is more to investing than meets the eye, and at this point a site that provides education can score.

Education is an area often neglected by online brokers. It should be graduated according to the level of sophisti-cation of the user, so that novices are not blinded with science and the experienced are not talked down to.

At StockAcademy there is full education provision that is, as noted earlier, often absent from other sites. The free courses, which are available to both customers and non-customers, are detailed and graded according to difficulty. They include not only workbook style material but also – on the basis that a picture is worth a thousand words – video clips illustrating many of the investing lessons to be learnt, as well as links to an online bookshop and reading list for further study.

Which broking site you choose is a matter of individual taste, but investors with the humility to recognise that they can always learn new techniques will find the provision of educational material, free of charge and linked to their broking site, is often of immense value.

Don't take my word for it. There are a number of sites that offer critical comparisons of broker sites, of which the best is probably Gomez (www.uk.gomez.com). One useful feature at the Gomez site is a tool that enables two brokers to be compared side by side.

Using this, and comparing one's existing broker with a possible alternative like StockAcademy, which was rated number one for ease of use, is a good way of concentrating the mind, particularly since the comparison includes both commission charges on a typical deal, but also some of the more qualitative factors.

Take control of your stock.

StockAcademy has made sharedealing simpler.

Access free financial education online, whatever your level of investment experience.

Activate your account in minutes and trade however you prefer; over the phone or online.

And for every trade you pay a flat rate of just £15*, no matter what its size.

Deal with StockAcademy and take control of your financial future.

stockacademy
A good deal simpler.

www.stockacademy.com
012 23 23 45 45

Financial Services Authority
25 The North Colonade
Canary Wharf
London E14 5HS
Tel: 0845 606 1234

London Stock Exchange
Public Information Department
Old Broad Street
London EC2N 1HP
Tel: 020 7797 1372

ProShare
Centurion House
24 Monument Street
London EC3R 8AQ
Tel: 020 7220 1730

Unit Trust Information Service
65 Kingsway
London WC2B 6TD
Tel: 020 8207 1361

Providers:

Bank of Scotland Investors Club
Ettrick House
37 South Gyle Crescent
Edinburgh EH12 9DS
Tel: 0845 600 4488
Web: www.bankofscotland.uk/investorsclub

Close Private Asset Management Limited
12 Appold Street
London EC2A 2AW
Tel: 020 7426 4000
Tel: 0161 935 8053
Web: www.cpam.co.uk

Credit Suisse Asset Management
Beaufort House
15 St Botolph Street
London EC3A 7JJ
Tel: 0800 389 1993
Web: csamfunds.co.uk

Gartmore Fund Managers Limited
Tel: 0800 289 336
Web: www.gartmore.com

Lifestyle Financial Services
Socially Responsible Investment Centre
Fourteen Wright Street
Kingston upon Hull
HU2 8HU
Tel: 0800 138 0851
Web: www.moneywells.col.uk

Moneygro Limited
Freepost LON 17217
15 Lanford Road
London SW15 1ZZ
Tel: 0800 169 5745
Web: www.moneygro.com

Popes Stockbrokers
15 Trinity Street
Hanley
Stoke on Trent
Staffordshire ST1 5PH
Tel: 01782 764000
Web: www.popes.co.uk

The Share Centre
Tel: 0800 800 008
Web: www.share.com

Since the early 1980's the personal savings and investment industry has undergone a period of almost constant change. Started by Michael Heseltine and the Financial Services Act in 1986, then continued by Margaret Thatcher with her Privatisation program, then the demutualisation of Building Societies during the late 1990's, investment has never been more accessible to more people, for very reasonable cost.

Big Bang in 1986 started the revolution, with the abolition of many archaic Stock Market regulations, but possibly most importantly it ended fixed commission rates. Stockbrokers now had to compete for business and the stockmarket was no longer the sole preserve of the very wealthy, or those with the right connections. This coupled with the then Government's sale of nationalised assets, creating a growing army of "Sids", so christened after the successful British Gas pre flotation ad campaign, awareness of the returns available from direct investment became greater than ever.

To date this has had two noticeable consequences, firstly share prices are a lot more volatile than they have ever been before as the weight of money flowing between stocks and markets has increased dramatically, and secondly the amount of information that is now available to investors. These consequences are inextricably linked, in that the more information that is available, the more investors may buy stocks, which may push prices up and ultimately lead to buying stocks that are too high and the creation of a speculative boom. Since 1986, this has significantly happened twice, ultimately leading to the dramatic fall in the market of 1987 and 2000. However the overall upward trend for shares is in tact and as with many things it is not merely having the information that is important it is the correct analysis of it, that can help investors to make money.

Much has been written about the dramatic rise between about October 1999 and March 2000 and equally dramatic subsequent fall, of all things Telecom, Media and Technology (TMT) related. During this time, companies with little or no value were valued firstly by the stock market in many millions, sometimes billions, of pounds, then equally quickly reversed to realistic levels. Many investors have lost money as a result of these falls, mainly due to the fact that traditional valuation methods of shares were temporarily forgotten, but ultimately all shares are valued on the basis of the future value of their business and how quickly this can be achieved.

All of which leads to the question of what is the role of the stockbroker today? Essentially there are three very distinct areas of business these days of which some firms specialise in just one, some like our own offer a personalised service across all three areas.

The most basic service that a stockbroker can off is an Execution Only dealing service, whereby a client researches his or her own ideas and then merely instructs their broker to buy or sell shares. These days this can be done on the Internet although to do so, does mean leaving some funds with the broker and any stock bought registered in their nominee company. Alternatively there are telephone services, local brokers can offer face to face dealing or even by post.

In past it may have been the case that potential clients felt intimidated and so would not dare to telephone the stockbroker directly, some choosing in some cases to deal through their banks instead. Those that have dealt through a stockbroker though have now got used to a very different service level. In many cases limits can be taken, deals are often executed at better than "best" prices, and of course and perhaps most important of all, advice can be given.

The advice given by stockbrokers, and for that matter any other financial institutions, needs to be based upon "suitability", and whether something is judged to be suitable needs to be based upon "know your client" information, which is normally collated at an initial meeting and needs to be updated regularly. The levels of advice can range from a client telephoning their broker wanting some reassurance that what they are about to do is sensible, to the client giving full discretion over the management of their investments to their broker.

Most portfolio management services offer the opportunity to leave the administration of the portfolio to professional managers. The management of the portfolio can be on an advisory basis but would normally be on a discretionary basis. The stockbroker will take care of all matters connected with the portfolio including investment decisions, income payments and give capital gains tax (CGT) guidance when possible. These services normally carry an annual management fee based upon the value of the portfolio, so as the fee will only increases if the portfolio value increases.

Alternatively, there are portfolio review services that provide advice and assistance on the setting up of a new portfolio to meet the client's specific needs, or advice on how an existing portfolio may be managed to ensure that the investments continue to meet the client's requirements, or merely regular valuations. In addition to daily advice that may be given, clients will normally be sent regular six monthly reviews and advice on corporate actions when they arise. These services normally carry a relatively small annual administration charge.

There are also a number of services now available for Investment Club, which are becoming increasingly popular for smaller investors. Each member will normally invest a small amount each month and these funds are then pooled and invested as one deal on behalf of all the members. This allows members to buy shares in individual companies at competitive dealing commission rates, when individually it would be uneconomic to do so. Investment Clubs usually hold monthly meetings to discuss the merits of their existing holdings and to consider any new investments. This allows members to use their collective knowledge to make investment decisions and so should help them make more informed choices. They can of course also be great fun.

In summary, the stockmarket has been and still should be a good source of capital growth. However, the individual companies' price movement are becoming more and more volatile and so the amounts to be gained and lost in the short term are increasing. This means that timing is becoming more important than ever before, but a good understanding of the increasingly available information should help you win more than you lose. However, if you do try to manage your own investments but without success, don't just give up, call your local stockbroker and discuss their services with them. I am sure that with their help your performance should soon pick up.

Richard Platt.

Richard Platt is a partner at Popes Stockbrokers, based in Stoke-on-Trent.

POPES
STOCKBROKERS 1870

Member of the London Stock Exchange.
Regulated by the Securities & Futures Authority.

We offer friendly and efficient stockbroking services at very competitive rates.

Call today and find out how easy it is to invest in the stockmarket.

Services include:

- Portfolio Management Service
- Portfolio Review Service
- Advisory Dealing Service
- Frequent Trader Service
- Execution-only Dealing Service
- Employee Dealing Service

We also offer:

- Investment Club facilities
- Self-select PEP's & ISA's
- Dealing in overseas stocks

Telephone: **01782 764000**

www.popes.co.uk

15 Trinity Street, Hanley, Stoke on Trent, Staffordshire ST1 5PH

StockAcademy
Tel: 012 23 23 45 45
Web: www.stockacademy.com

Wesleyan Assurance Society
Colmore Circus
Birmingham B4 6AR
Tel: 0800 0680 680
Web: www.wesleyan.co.uk

Traded endowment policies (TEPs)

Further information:

Association of Policy Market Makers
Tel: 020 7739 3949

Market makers:

Beale Dobie & Co Ltd
Fullbridge Mill
Maldon
Essex CM9 5FN
Tel: 01621 851133

PolicyPlus International
King's Court
Bath BA1 1ER
Tel: 0845 055 3123
Web: www.policyplus.com

Don't Surrender - Sell for more

Bath based PolicyPlus, one of the leading market makers in the Traded Endowment Policy (TEP) market, has been buying and selling endowments since 1989. The market has grown considerably during that period and is likely to continue to expand as life companies are encouraged to notify policyholders that selling on the TEP market is an attractive alternative to surrendering their policy.

Selling

If you have decided to surrender your endowment policy – don't. PolicyPlus could offer you much more than the surrender value. For more information, visit **www.policyplus.com**, call **0845 055 3123** for a free quote or talk to your Independent Financial Adviser.

Investing

For buyers, TEPs are an alternative investment to use in financial planning. TEPs are medium to long-term investments with high guarantees provided by the accrued value of the policy. They have fixed maturity dates and are an efficient means of planning for major future costs such as school fees, weddings or retirement. For advice on investing in TEPs, contact an Independent Financial Adviser.

PolicyPlus' website at **www.policyplus.com** offers an informative and straightforward guide to buying and selling endowment policies.

PolicyPlus International plc is King's Court, Bath BA1 1ER.

Regulated by the Personal Investment Authority.

Appendix II

Independent Financial Advisers (IFAs)

Regulators and further information:

Financial Services Authority
25 The North Colonade
Canary Wharf
London E14 5HS
Tel: 0845 606 1234

Financial Services Ombudsman
South Quay Plaza,
183 Marshwall
London, E14 9SR
Tel: 0845 080 1800

IFA Promotion Ltd
17–19 Emery Road
Brislington
Bristol BS4 5PF
Tel: 0117 971 1177

The Money Management National Register of Fee-based Advisers
172 Drury Lane
London WC2B 5QR
Tel: 020 7074 1200

Solicitors for Independent Financial Advice
10 East Street
Epsom
Surrey KT17 1HH
Tel: 01372 721172

Providers:

Ace Insurance and Financial Services Ltd
1a Kilburn Bridge
Kilburn High Road
London W1N 9AE
Tel: 0207 493 8360
Fax: 0207 493 8361

Andrew Copeland Financial Services Ltd
230 Portland Road
London SE25 4SL
Tel: 020 8656 8435
Fax: 020 8655 1271
Web: www.service@andrewcopeland.co.uk

Ashley Law Ltd
30–32 Stains Road
Hounslow TW3 3LZ
Tel: 0500 104 106
Web: www.ashleylaw.co.uk

Chelsea Financial Services
Tel: 0800 0713333
Web: www.chelseafs.co.uk

Personal Touch Finance
Tel: 01564 206250
Web: www.theinsurancesupermarket.com

PERSONAL TOUCH FINANCE

If you have not already heard about us, Personal Touch Finance is a well-established, originally family run, company based in the West Midlands. We now offer a full and comprehensive range of independent financial advice through a nationwide network of advisers. Our Head Office has 70 experienced staff that are consistently trained and updated on the changes taking place in the market place. We are based at Cheshire House, High Street, Knowle, West Midlands B93 0LL.

As a Company, we are dedicated to providing an outstanding quality of service. We are not perfect, but we strive to be the best. We recognise that customers are at the heart of our business and therefore take pride in providing a service built on a relationship of innovation, trust and partnership.

Our many professional advisers will be happy to provide you with confidential advice for both your own personal financial needs as well as those of your company.

- Competitively priced Life Insurance
- Up to date information on a wide range of investments and the companies that provide them
- Technical advice on Trust and Inheritance Tax Planning
- We can help you with Retirement Planning (including stakeholder pensions)
- We can source the best mortgage on the marketplace for you*
- We can offer you a totally independent general insurance service for buildings, contents, car, etc.*

* These products are not regulated by the Personal Investment Authority

This comprehensive service has grown out of the large investment we have made in acquiring advanced technology, including a computerised back office administration system and 'state of the art' software packages to source the best deals around. We are continually developing new products and creating market leaders. By contacting us, we can assure you that you will have access to all the best packages available at the touch of a button backed up by that 'personal touch' of friendly and helpful staff.

For more information you can visit our website.
www.theinsurancesupermarket.com

Alternatively, please telephone us on
01564 206250
and ask for Richard.

Personal Touch Finance is a trading style of
Personal Touch Insurance Services Ltd
which is regulated by the
Personal Investment Authority

Professional Financial Services
Trafalgar House
11 Waterloo Place, SW1Y
Tel: 0207 930 4619

Torquil Clark
Tel: 0800 413186
Web: tqonline.co.uk

Appendix III

Insurers – general, life and home

Regulators & further information:

Association of British Insurers
51 Gresham Street
London, EC2V 7HQ
Tel: 020 7600 3333

Financial Ombudsman Service
South Quay Plaza,
183 Marshwall
London, E14 9SR
Tel: 0845 080 1800

General Insurance Standards Council
110 Cannon Street
London, EC4N 6EU
Tel: 020 7648 7800

Providers:

Admiral
Admiral House
38–42 Newport Road
Cardiff, CF2 1XX
Tel: 0800 600 800
Web: www.admiral.co.uk

A-Plan Assurance
Tel: 0800 172172
Web: www.a-planlife.co.uk

LIFE INSURANCE that is HONEST, FAIR and GREAT VALUE FOR MONEY......ARE YOU KIDDING?

Let's face it, life insurance sales representatives have never really had a good image, but perhaps now this is changing...

A-Plan Assurance is an impartial life insurance intermediary, which delivers low cost life cover via top brand insurance companies without fees, cancellation charges or any other hidden costs. Even the telephone call is completely free of charge!

Using the latest technology, A-Plan will obtain prices from many of the leading insurance companies, swiftly and without fuss, presenting all of their findings to their customers so that they can choose which ever is best.

Deceptively sold pensions, endowment shortfalls, commission-hungry salesmen trying to push everything under the sun when all you require is simple mortgage protection, are all images that are conjured up when people think of Life Insurance. Even worse, these emotions often detract from the importance of the product and prevent many from protecting themselves and their loved ones. Consequently, millions of UK citizens are left either very under-insured or totally unprotected.

If something happened to you or your partner what realistic quality of life would you or your family be able to lead? Would you really be able to maintain the same lifestyle or anywhere near it?

Now you can with confidence.

A-Plan Assurance can help you protect your loved ones without fear of charges, hassle, or of being ripped off, and give you great savings.

*Top Brands:- Norwich Union, Legal & General, Standard Life, Scottish Widows and many more.

*_No_ Charges or Obligation:- No costs are ever incurred by the customer for the service provided. Not at the outset or throughout the term of the plan.

*_No_ Hassle and _Free_ to call:- Applications can be completed at your leisure at home or then and there on the telephone.

*Impartial & Professional Staff:- Salary paid, not commission based advisors.

Take a look at these two examples -

Mr Sutherland & Miss Stafford from Farnborough had quotations from a direct sales force to protect their mortgage. A-Plan arranged a joint mortgage protection term assurance, with critical illness cover, resulting in a saving of £136 each month compared to what the competitor had quoted them to protect the same mortgage. Over the 25 years of the policy this would amount to a massive saving of £40,800.

"All round the service and information given was very helpful" **B Sutherland, Hants**

"Following my telephone conversation with you today, I had to write and say how pleased I am with the quote you gave for Life and Critical Illness cover. Of all the companies I contacted, A-Plan Assurance was without doubt the most competitive and will definitely save me a lot of money. I was very happy with the service and advice I was given by your representative." **Annette Irving, Kent**

Call us now on:- 0800-172-172

A-Plan Assurance is a trading style of Assured Futures Limited which are regulated by the Personal Investment Authority. Some types of Life Insurance are not regulated

Bupa
Web: www.bupa.co.uk

Canada Life Assurance Co.
3rd Floor, Centre Heights
137 Finchley Rd
Swiss Cottage
London NW3
Tel: 020 722 6563
Web: www.canadalife.com

Copeland Insurance
Andrew Copeland Financial Services Ltd
230 Portland Road
London SE25 4SL
Tel: 020 8656 8435
Fax: 020 8655 1271
Web: www.service@andrewcopeland.co.uk

CGNU
1 Lloyds Avenue
London EC3N
Tel: 020 626 8711
Web: www.norwichunion-direct.co.uk

Congregational & General Insurance plc
Currer Street
Bradford BD1 5BA
Tel: 01274 700700
Web: www.congregational.co.uk

Cornhill Direct 50+
Direct Ins Div, Great Park House
Great Park Rd
Bradley Stoke
Bristol BS32 4QG
Tel: Freephone: 0800 60 70 70
Web: www.cornhilldirect.co.uk

Dial Direct
Dial Direct House
Corporation Street
Coventry, CV1 1GY
Tel: Car Insurance: 0800 068 8001
Home Insurance: 0800 068 8003
Web: www.ddirect.co.uk

Direct Line
Tel: 0845 246 8674
Web: www.directline.com

Eagle Star Direct
60 St Mary Ave
London EC3A 8JQ
Tel: 0800 333 800
Web: www.eaglestar.co.uk

Endsleigh Insurance Services
Shurdington Rd.
Cheltenham
Gloucestershire
GL51 4UE
Tel: Life Insurance: 0800 028 6271
Tel: Motor Insurance: 0800 028 3571
Web: www.endsleigh.co.uk

The Finance Surgery
Tel: 0800 018 1099

Friendly Life
Tel: 0800 195 9812
Web: www.friendlylife.co.uk

A good home insurance deal from your mortgage provider?

Don't bank on it.

Cutting out the middlemen could save you up to 30%.

Banks and building societies can take commission on home insurance. So why not cut out the middleman and go direct? Call Direct Line and we could save you up to 30% on your buildings and contents insurance... with **no hassle, no hidden charges and no commission.**

- *Approved by major banks and building societies*
- *We aim to cut premiums, not the quality of cover*
- *We'll pay any switching fees up to £25*
- *No complicated forms to fill in - we'll do it for you over the phone*
- *Over 950,000 householders trust us for their home insurance cover*

Call us now for a quotation

0845 246 8674

or buy online **www.directline.com**

DIRECT LINE

Direct Line Insurance and the telephone on wheels are the trademarks of Direct Line Insurance plc. Direct Line House, 3 Edridge Road, Croydon CR9 1AG. Member of the General Insurance Standards Council. Terms and conditions apply. Calls may be monitored or recorded.

Insurance & Investment Solutions
10 Kendal Street
Kendal
LA9 4AD
Tel: 0800 970 0457
Web: www.lifedirect.com

Jackson Lee Underwriting Ltd
Freepost
SEA4077
Carshalton SM5 4BR
Tel: 020 8255 2100
Fax: 020 8773 0406

Legal & General Group plc.
Temple Court
11 Queen Victoria St.
London EC4N
Tel: 0207 528 6200
Web: www.legal-and-general.co.uk

Life Direct
Insurance & Investment Solutions
Tel: 0800 970 0457
Web: www.lifedirect.com

LifeSearch
Tel: 0800 316 3166
Web: www.lifesearch.co.uk

Marks & Spencer Financial Services
Chester Business Park
CH99 9FB
Tel: 0800 363 422
Web: www.marksandspencer.co.uk

Experienced driver?
Enjoy lower premiums
with Cornhill motor insurance

At Cornhill we believe experienced drivers should be rewarded with lower premiums – rather than penalised for the mistakes of younger motorists.

That's why Cornhill motor cover has been designed with drivers aged 50+ especially in mind – backed by the service quality you'd expect from one of Britain's leading motor insurers.

If you're aged 50 or over **visit our website on:**

www.cornhilldirect.co.uk

or call free on **0800 60 70 70** and quote ref: FFL01, to find out how you can save money on your motor insurance AND enjoy valuable extra benefits including:

- **FREE** 24 hour legal helpline
- **FREE** car audio replacement
- **FREE** accident recovery
- **FREE** courtesy car*

Calls may be recorded. We may not be able to quote in all circumstances. (*comprehensive cover only – conditions apply)

CORNHILL
Direct
Deliver the Promise

Opening hours
Monday to Friday
8am – 8pm,
Saturday 9am – 3pm

Cornhill Insurance PLC is a member of the General Insurance Standards Council

ARE ALL THE BRICKS IN YOUR WALL?

by Derek J. Mauri, *ACII*

Managing Director of Jackson Lee Underwriting Ltd

It is generally accepted that the largest and most important transaction that anyone enters into during their lifetime is the purchase of a home. Not only is it important but, apparently, apart from divorce, it is also the most stressful event you will encounter.

After having dodged gazumping, gone through the torment of estate agent hype, surveyor delay, mortgage arranger cramp, lawyer paralysis and removal operative blunder, in the end you find yourself bloodied but unbowed, weary but wiser, in your own home where you can relax safe in the knowledge that your home is your castle, a bastion against all that fate can devise for your discomfort, because, exercising proper prudence, have you not taken care to put in place the ultimate protection by insuring the fabric of the building, and its contents, against all the usual perils, and some unusual ones as well? Everything has been covered. Or has it?

It is remarkable how often what is arguably the most crucial insurance available in connection with home ownership is neglected – the insurance that covers the very foundation that makes home ownership possible – the continuity of your earning capacity and, therefore, your ability to keep making the repayments on the mortgage.

The concept of a 'job for life' is now outdated. Multi-company experience is today a positive requirement for career advancement and ambition must also negotiate a fluctuating economic climate often necessitating changes in career path! And between these changes there will undoubtedly be unplanned periods of unemployment. At such times it would be comforting to know that whatever problems being without a job might bring, being unable to keep making the repayments on your mortgage and running the risk of losing your home will not be one of them.

Likewise, while it is an accepted fact that the upwardly mobile young are immortal, it is amazing how even the shortest period of illness can play havoc with future plans – the receipt of foreclosure papers while lying in bed with your leg up can be a significant impediment to recovery.

Why then do so relatively few mortgage payers take mortgage protection insurance? Is it too expensive? Not really! Mortgage protection is, in fact, remarkably inexpensive. However, if the only consideration that you have made has been on the basis of the cover offered by your mortgage provider then it might well appear to be more expensive than it need be. Shop around – this cover does not have to be expensive – as a study of the advertisements will reveal.

Cost is, of course, important but it should not be the sole criteria to be considered in selecting your protection policy. A cheap contract which requires you to wait 90 days or even longer before it pays your claim could be a false economy when compared with one, possibly costing a little more, that pays from the First Day of your claim!

What are the considerations to be taken into account when choosing your Mortgage Protection insurance?

What cover do I need? If you have a job which, on disability occurring, pays a good period of full pay followed by a similar period of half pay, then disability (accident & sickness) cover may not be the greatest imperative. In this case your overriding requirement would be for unemployment cover – your need is therefore for an insurer, like Jackson Lee, who will write unemployment cover on its own.

How long must I wait before a claim is paid? The 'waiting period' is the time that must elapse after you become ill, injured or unemployed before payment of benefit under the insurance begins. Generally this is 30 days but exercise caution some contracts have significantly longer periods which, for the unwary, can spin out to as long as 120 days before a payment is made!

Do I get anything for the waiting period? Not always but under my company's *Loanstar* contract once your illness, injury or unemployment has lasted for 30 days a full monthly payment of benefit is made on day 31 followed by payment for every day of disability or unemployment which follows, effectively ensuring that once you have been unable to work for 30 days you are paid for every day of your disability or unemployment – BACK TO DAY ONE!

How long will a claim be paid for? Twelve months is the usual maximum period that a claim will be paid.

When must I start paying premiums? The payment of the first premium generally puts the cover under an insurance policy into force. However, recognising the expense of buying a first home, or moving from one to another, many insurers alleviate that expense by offering an initial premium free period. See how many months your prospective insurer offers after commencement of cover before you are required to start paying.

When will a claim not be paid? In common with most insurances Mortgage Protection contracts have their terms and conditions and there are circumstances when a claim will not be paid. Unemployment benefit will not be paid if it arises from voluntary redundancy or if you knew that you were to be made redundant when you took the insurance out. Unemployment occurring soon after the contract is taken out, usually 90 days, sometimes more, sometimes less, is not covered for how ever long it might continue. Also, if you are a contract employee it would be wise to check how the circumstances of your employment might be viewed by your insurer should you lose your job.

On the health side pregnancy is not covered although complication arising from it would be. Cover for accident is immediate but sickness within the first 30 days is usually excluded. Disability from something you suffered from before you took the policy out is likely to be excluded although this is often limited, so if you have an existing problem check how your prospective insurer views pre-existing conditions. Claims arising from back problems or stress and depression are closely investigated but evidence of treatment by a specialist is usually sufficient for insurers to agree payment.

For every one who blesses the day they took out mortgage protection insurance there are many more who rue the day that they didn't. From the point of view of an insurer comment can only be made about our customers, those who are insured. Alison, for instance. After many months of planning and saving with her partner, they bought a small house and, together set about making a home. As mortgages go

theirs was not a large one but within the limits of their joint earnings, her as an office worker and him as a trainee, it was the maximum they could prudently borrow. Redundancy came as a shock to Alison but the payment she received from her mortgage protection policy allowed her to maintain her contribution to the building society payments, ensuring that not too many of their plans had to be put on hold during the six months it took her to find a suitable new job.

Then there was Barry. The arrival of his second child indicated the need for larger accommodation. That safely achieved everything looked rosy – until his accident – severed tendons are not conducive to the butcher's trade but he is recovering and looking forward to an early return to work, happy that during his forced inactivity when no work has meant no income, the roof over his family's heads has been secure, not one repayment to the building society being missed thanks to his mortgage protection policy.

A similar story can be told about every claim that crosses any insurer's desk. When the unexpected happens will you be an Alison or Barry? Or will you be one of those who thought they were fireproof?

Insurance is no different to any other service or commodity changes and improvements continually occur. It is not true that mortgage protection can only be obtained at the start of your mortgage. Mortgages in payment can be covered – without difference in cost or terms and conditions. So, if you have mortgage protection insurance check that it has not been overtaken by recent developments. If it has now may be the time to make a change and select the contract that is better and, perhaps, more economical for your circumstances.

If you are not insured then it's later than you think! Remember cover is not expensive – shop around – tomorrow might be too late!

Jackson Lee Underwriting Limited is a third party administration company providing services to certain syndicates at Lloyd's and other insurers. Jackson Lee was established specifically to administer Mortgage Payment Protection, as well as creditor or loan payment protection insurances. Our operations are controlled and authorised under the terms of Binding Authorities granted to us by the various underwriting syndicates to whom we provide administration services.

CONGREGATIONAL & GENERAL INSURANCE PLC

Founded in 1891, Congregational & General, insures over 4,500 places of worship of all denominations, as well as homes and businesses. In 1994 the Company became a wholly owned subsidiary of the Congregational & General Charitable Trust, which disburses grants to charitable causes, churches and schools.

The Congregational provides a choice of products, backed by a flexible underwriting approach ensuring all policyholders continually receive value for money. Our Church Choice and Business Choice policies offer a range of cover that can be tailored to individual requirements.

Home Choice is our sum-insured household policy and 'nest' offers competitive rates for 3 & 4 bedroom properties. Both provide cover for Buildings and Contents together, or in isolation, for all the standard perils, with optional cover available – including Business Equipment and Legal Protection.

Home Choice has a nil excess on buildings (Subsidence £1,000) and you can save up to 45% with a range of discounts including No Claims and Maturity.

The standard cover on Nest also includes Accidental Damage for both Buildings and Contents, as well as All Risks cover for personal possessions and money away from the home.

There is an extensive range of helplines, including Home Assistance and Tax Advice Services, available to all policyholders and our staff is dedicated to help and support customers in the event of a claim. The Congregational aims to provide a unique, personal service to our policyholders, ensuring the highest standards of customer care, through the commitment, enthusiasm and technical skill of our dedicated staff.

Norwich Union Direct
8 Surrey Street
Norwich NR1 3NG
Tel: 0800 056 5083
Fax: 0208 551 4530
Web: www.norwich-union.co.uk

Personal Touch Insurance
Tel: 01564 206280
Web: www.personaltouchinsurance.com

Prudential
142 Holborn Bars, London
EC1N 2NH
Tel: 0800 300 300
Web: www.pru.co.uk

Royal & Sun Alliance
Property Investors Unit
77 Shaftesbury Avenue
London W1V
Tel: 0207 734 7211
Web: www.royal-and-sunalliance.com

Saga Services Ltd.
The Saga Building
Middelburg Square
Folkestone
Kent CT20 1AZ
Tel: 01483 553 553

Scottish Widows
Direct Sales
PO Box 17037
69 Morrison Street
Edinburgh EH3 8YD
Tel: 0845 845 1002
Web: www.scottishwidows.co.uk

Standard Life Assurance
Standard Life House
30 Lothian Rd
Edinburgh EH1 2DH
Tel: 0845 60 60 100
Web: www.standardlife.co.uk

Sun Life
107 Cheapside
London EC2V 6DU
Tel: 0117 989 3000
Web: www.sunlife.co.uk

Western Provident Association
Rivergate House
Blackbrook Park
Taunton TA1 2PE
Tel: 0800 783 3 783
Web: www.wpahealth.co.uk

Zurich Insurance Co.
The Zurich Building
90 Fenchurch St.
London EC3M
Tel: 0207 702 4550
Web: www.zurich.com

Appendix IV

Buying & Selling Property

Mortgage lenders and brokers

Abbey National
Abbey House
Baker Street
London NW1 6XL
Freephone: 0800 555 100

Creditweb
Tel: 0800 359 3388
Web: creditweb.com

First Mortgage Direct
Homepurchase: 0800 731 4298
Remortgage: 0800 389 5371
Web: www.firstmortgage.co.uk

Freephone Mortgages
Tel: 08000 15 15 36

Halifax
Trinity Road
Halifax HX1 2RG
Tel: 0800 20 30 49

LET'S TALK MORTGAGES

In times like these when equity markets are shaky, people look for investment opportunities that offer security. Forget the get rich quick claims that characterised dot.com mania: what we want now is steady income, reliable capital growth and tangible assets. In short, property.

The problem of course is that while your nest egg may represent a handsome portfolio of shares, it would scarcely buy the broom cupboard of a des res in the right area – and location, as we know, is the first, second and third most important thing about a residential property. The solution, is to use mortgage borrowing to make your capital work harder. What's interesting, is that while this was always an option, the market used to be loaded against the investor, with lenders charging premium rates. Now, both mainstream and specialist lenders have jumped on the bandwagon, offering the sorts of deals and rates that we're used to for residential mortgages.

Some specifics to bear in mind if you're thinking of borrowing to buy an investment property are these.

FIRST, while the amount that you can borrow for a residential mortgage is usually based on a multiple of your income, when you buy-to-let, what matters is the rent that the property can command. Lenders will want the monthly rental income to more than cover the monthly mortgage payment – the cushion will be between 25% and 40%.

SECOND, you'll need a deposit of at least 15%. In the buy-to-let world, there are no 100% mortgages.

THIRD, although you won't need to provide all the personal detail that's required when you take out a residential loan, some lenders will insist that you can show annual income of at least £20,000.

A recent variant which you might consider if you're moving house but want to invest at the same time, is the let-to buy mortgage. A lender will advance up to 90% of the value of your house which you then let while buying a new property to live in.

If you want to buy more than one property, some lenders offer portfolio schemes. In these, you can arrange up to £1m of borrowing in a single process, and before you actually buy the properties.

The buy-to-let market, has grown so rapidly, and competition for business is so strong, that it makes sense to get advice from an independent broker before diving in.

Let's Talk Mortgages, based in London's Belsize Park, prides itself on offering advice not just on the right buy-to-let mortgage but on providing the complete package including buildings insurance and redundancy protection, as well as being able to recommend solicitors who are familiar with the processes. We can also, through sister company Eton Square Financial Management, advise on fitting property investment into a complete financial strategy. After all, you can't just follow fashion if you really want your money to be as safe as houses.

Let's talk Mortgages...

- **Large Loan Specialists**
- **Self-Employed with or without accounts**
- **CCJ's, Defaults, Bankruptcy, IVA's**
- **Mortgages & Remortgages - Reduce Monthly Payments**
- **Capital Raising / Debt Consolidation**
- **No proof of income / Self Certification to 90%**
- **Buy to Let - from 15% deposit**

Call Free on
0800 0856 729

Your home is at risk if you do not keep up the payments on a mortgage or other loans secured on it.

Finance for Life

THE majority of investors south of, say, Birmingham, would probably need a road atlas to even find where Leek is...

But the Staffordshire Moorlands mill town's homegrown building society has been steadily putting itself on the map for almost 140 years.

And despite occasionally being confused with Leeds United Football Club, LEEK United proudly remains one of Britain's few mutual societies, placing the interests of its fiercely loyal customer base before profiteering for external shareholders.

The friendlier face of finance serves all its savers and homeowner's financial needs from 12 branches throughout Cheshire, Staffordshire, Shropshire and Staffordshire, and a network of agencies.

And its regular inclusion in the national press Best Buy tables ensure an even wider market for its range of high quality, value-for-money products – including the Leeks attractive Buy To Let mortgage.

Created in spring 1863 as the Leek United Permanent Benefit Building Society, the Leeks reputation was built on the motto Firm and Lasting (symbolised by the pyramids). More than a century later, the pyramid still stands as the Society's distinctive green logo, while Leek Uniteds traditionally high standards of personal service remain stronger than ever.

That same Egyptian theme continues to capture the imaginations of generations of new young savers through the Leek's cuddly mascot, Humphrey the Camel. Humphrey has his own savings account, the popular Humphrey Club, for children under the age of 11, and he is a familiar figure at many of the Society's charity fund-raising and community events.

To find out more about Leek Uniteds range of competitive, high quality financial services and products, call (01538) 384151 now – or simply log on and browse the Society's website: www.leekunited.co.uk

For further information, contact:
Pauline Roessler, Marketing Manager, on (01538) 384151
Martin Bell, Press/PR, on (01782) 710281.

Leek United
BUILDING SOCIETY

The *friendlier* face of finance

Mortgages

Open the door to a solid investment with our Buy to Let† mortgage

Call today for details

50 St. Edward Street   Leek   Staffordshire   ST13 5DH
Tel: 01538 384151   email: mort.apps@leekunited.co.uk
www.leekunited.co.uk
Free*fone* 0800 093 0004

Choosing a mortgage used to be one of the less stressful parts of buying a home. Mortgages on offer from banks and building societies were all pretty much the same. That has all changed now. There is a growing number of mortgage lenders in the UK – around 150 at last count. And, each of these can typically offer up to 20 different types of mortgage deals. The choice of mortgage is enormous, and daunting. This is where **MORTGAGE TALK DIRECT** can help.

MORTGAGE TALK provides specialist independent Mortgage Advice. We offer assistance on almost every aspect of the house buying market, including first time buying, investment properties and properties to let and re-mortgaging.

When purchasing a new home you should look to arrange your mortgage as early as possible. It can take a few weeks to process a mortgage application, and it is important that the person selling the property know you are in a position to move quickly. The amount you can borrow is based on your income, your status, the deposit, and the affordability of the proposed monthly repayments. To assist you with this and put you in the strongest possible position when viewing properties **MORTGAGE TALK DIRECT** are able to give a decision in principle on an amount you need to borrow within 24 hours. We then produce a mortgage certificate showing your agreed mortgage amount that can be used when shopping around.

The next step is easy. When you have found a property simply contact **MORTGAGE TALK**, and one of our fully qualified advisers will ask you a series of questions. From this they will be able to advise you of the most suitable mortgage available to meet your needs. The necessary application forms will then be completed and forward to you for checking and signing. Once returned they will be passed to a dedicated administrator who will contact you, your solicitor and Estate Agent with regular updates until your mortgage has completed.

As well as saving you time and effort **MORTGAGE TALK DIRECT** also offers free of charge Buyers Cost Protection. Whilst we hope that your purchase will go through smoothly, things can sometimes go wrong. The seller may lose his purchase and have to pull out from the sale to you, they may change their minds about selling, suffer a change of circumstances or accept a higher offer for their property from someone else.

If this happens you are normally left having to pay the legal costs and the mortgage valuation fee in respect of the lost purchase and have no means of recovering them. However, if you make your mortgage application through **MORTGAGE TALK DIRECT**, and your purchase falls through for a qualifying reason on that property, we will refund lost legal fees (including disbursements and VAT) up to a maximum of £150 and you will be issued with a voucher entitling you to a free scheme one valuation, up to a limit of £250 on your next mortgage.

All this is done from the comfort of your own home, and at a time convenient for you. To find out more contact us now on **0845 600 4002** or visit our website at **www.mortgagetalk.co.uk.**

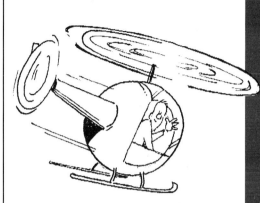

There's the hard way... and there's the easy way.

1500–2000 products from all major lenders available to you direct.

Talk
Mortgage
direct

A revolution in the Mortgage Market

One local call to search the market.

0845 600 400 2

Independent Mortgage Advice
www.mortgagetalk.co.uk

Independent Mortgage Brokerage
18 Exeter Street
Covent Garden
London WC2E 7DU
Tel: 020 7836 8448

Charcol
Tel: 0800 708 191
Web: www.charcolonline.co.uk

Leek United Building Society
50 St. Edward Street
Leek
Staffordshire ST13 5DH
Tel: 0800 093 0004
Web: www.leekunited.co.uk

Let's Talk Mortgages
Tel: 0800 0856 729

Mortgage Talk Direct
Tel: 0845 600 4002
Web: www.mortgagetalk.co.uk

Northern Rock
Northern Rock House
Gosforth
Newcastle upon Tyne
NE3 4PL
Tel: Mortgages: 0845 60 50 500
Tel: Investments: 0845 600 4466
Web: www.northernrock.co.uk

Standard Life Bank
Standard Life House
30 Lothian Road
Edinburgh EH1 2DH
Tel: 0845 845 8450

THE MORTGAGE MAZE MADE EASY

Buying a home is one of the biggest decisions we have to make in life - not only do we want to find the house of our dreams but we have to be able to afford it - and that often means getting a mortgage.

Searching for a mortgage these days is no easy task, in fact with more than 5000 mortgages available to choose from, its not a case of one size fits all - so where do you start?

Many people speak to friends and relatives to hear their experiences, others may go and visit their bank to see what they have on offer. This however, can often confuse the process more, as what may have been the right mortgage or lender for someone else may not necessarily mean it's right for you. So, to really get the full picture of what's available, borrowers need to speak to someone who can give them both advice and help to unravel the choices and decisions that need to be made. The first point of call should be to seek out professional mortgage advice.

These days professional mortgage advice can be sought in many ways. Banks and Building Societies can advise you on their own products and services or, if you seek help from a professional mortgage adviser it will be likely you will be advised on a much wider variety of mortgage products. However, some will charge a fee for their services and others may only be able to select from a restricted panel of lenders and therefore will not offer a completely independent view. There is an alternative solution however, available from companies such as Creditweb.

Creditweb is a telephone and internet based mortgage broker which enables customers to search and apply for mortgages online or over the telephone, whichever way suits them best. It gives borrowers access to the whole mortgage market; enabling them to search for a mortgage from the wide choice of products available from every UK mortgage lender. In addition, it also offers access to 'best of breed', and exclusive market leading mortgage products, which have been specially negotiated with leading banks and building societies and are only available via Creditweb.

Creditweb has been developed around the needs of home buyers and recognises the difficulties facing borrowers looking for a mortgage. It aims to equip them, whether they are first time buyers, remortgaging or simply wanting to move house, with everything they might need to make finding the right mortgage as easy and simple as possible.

But Creditweb gives borrowers the ability to do far more than simply view mortgage information online. Borrowers can also consult, via the phone, an experienced Creditweb mortgage adviser who will select the most appropriate product for their needs. The advice is completely independent and free of charge and there is no requirement to purchase additional products and services.

Using the Creditweb site (www.creditweb.co.uk) borrowers are able to find the best deals with the minimum effort. Borrowers can access detailed product information from the Creditweb home page with only two clicks of the mouse.

By using its expertise, Creditweb identifies the 'best buy' mortgages available from the entire mortgage market - these are then checked on a daily basis to make sure they are still the best available and displayed on the site. When selecting best buy products, Creditweb takes into consideration factors such as early redemption charges, the ability to upgrade products, compulsory insurance requirements and fees.

The Creditweb site focus's on best buy products, because feedback continually indicates that borrowers are usually unwilling to complete lengthy questionnaires on-line simply to enable them to view product tables. Creditweb therefore gives borrowers easy access to 'best buy' product information, with the option for Creditweb to carry out a full search on their behalf, of the entire mortgage market using their own personal details.

The Creditweb site also offers a host of other facilities to help ensure that making mortgage decisions is a much smoother and easier process. Borrowers can use monthly repayment and maximum loan calculators to determine the optimum size mortgage for their financial circumstances and print an application form from their own computer. They will also benefit from a fast and efficient service with access to on-site underwriters and direct links to a number of leading lenders, thus ensuring borrowers applications do not experience unnecessary delays.

Creditweb is fully committed to the Mortgage Code and will therefore present information on its website in a way which is easy for borrowers to directly compare one product with another, make all the terms of a product clear and easy to understand and be completely impartial in the advice it gives. Creditweb will also fully inform borrowers about all fees or charges they may be required to pay by the lender before they apply for a loan.

The mortgage process can be made so much easier by using Creditweb, There are no lengthy two hour interviews and endless forms to complete, there is complete objectivity, ensuring the needs of the borrowers are met and what's more - it all for free!

Life can be challenging enough and finding the most suitable mortgage need not be yet another mountain to climb. Let someone else do all the hard work and you can relax in the knowledge that Creditweb will act on your behalf to ensure all your needs are met to help you obtain the home you really want.

It seems to good to be true, but its actually not - so why not give it try? If you have found a mortgage you are interested in or are in the process of searching for one - give Creditweb a call or have a look at the website and see what you think. Creditweb will find the mortgage for you, they will ensure you have all the relevant forms to fill in and will ensure the mortgage process is as smooth as it can possibly be.

Give Creditweb a call on 0800 358 5588 or visit their website at www.creditweb.co.uk

Yorkshire Bank plc
Tel: 0800 20 21 22
Web: www.YBonline.co.uk

Estate agents, solicitors and surveyors

Regulators and sources of further information:

Council for Licensed Conveyances (CLC)
16 Glebe Road
Chelmsford
Essex CM1 1QG
Tel: 01245 349 599

The Incorporated Society of Valuers and Auctioneers
3 Cadogan Gate
London SW1X 0AS
Tel: 0207 235 2282

The Law Society
113 Chancery Lane
London
WC2A 1PL
Tel: 020 7242 1222

The Law Society of Scotland
The Law Society's Hall
26 Drumsheugh Gardens
Edinburgh EH3 7YR
Tel: 0131 226 7411

The Law Society of Northern Ireland
Law Society House
98 Victoria Street
Belfast BT1 3JZ
Tel: 028 9023 1614

The National Association of Estate Agents
Arbon House
21 Jury Street
Warwick CV34 4EH
Tel: 01926 496 800

The Ombudsman for Estate Agents
Becket House
4 Bridge Street
Salisbury
Wiltshire SP1 2LX
Tel: 01722 333306

The Royal Institution of Chartered Surveyors
12 Great George Street
Parliament Square
London SW1P 3AD
Tel: 020 7222 7000

Buying and selling property overseas

Andrew Copeland Financial Services Ltd
230 Portland Road
London SE25 4SL
Tel: 020 8656 8435
Fax: 020 8655 1271
Web: www.service@andrewcopeland.co.uk

Florida USA Direct Ltd
29 Tudor Way
Wickford
Essex SS12 0HS
Tel: 0870 753 567 432

Halewood International Foreign Exchange
Tel: 01753 859159
Web: www.hifx.co.uk

Overseas Homes and Investments Ltd
The Aztec Centre
Aztec West
Bristol BS32 4TD
Tel: 01454 203 450
Fax: 01454 203 451

FLORIDA

widest choice of luxury homes with private pools in exclusive communities
within minutes of Disney - many in frontline golf course positions

ORLANDO - DISNEY

Choice of rental schemes
offering excellent
investment returns

Full management and
letting service

80% mortgages available
subject to status

Low cost inspection visits

As an independent group, at Superior Homes we promise to provide every one of our customers with accurate and unbiased advice concerning every aspect of home purchase and ownership in Florida and Spain. Our friendly and dedicated staff are always available to answer your questions in a thoroughly professional manner. We aim to provide an unrivalled service to ensure your future satisfaction.

PROPERTY SALES ♦ PROJECT DEVELOPMENT ♦ MANAGEMENT ♦ RENTALS

SPAIN

white sandy beaches, crystal clear water, fragrant orange groves and sunny skies - your new dream home awaits you at

OLIVA NOVA GOLF

Oliva Nova Golf lies directly on the coast near Denia on Spain's sunny Costa Blanca and is surrounded by unspoilt natural landscape and fine white sandy beaches.

The quality and value of the homes at Oliva Nova Golf are exceptional and include studios, apartments, town homes and villas. On-site facilities include a championship golf course, 4 star luxury hotel, restaurants, shops, bank and numerous water sports and leisure activities.

3 day inspection visits from only £79.00 per person incl. flight, accommodation and meals.

THOUGHT ABOUT SPENDING WINTER IN A SUMMER CLIMATE?

Florida USA Direct Ltd is a medium sized company specialising in selling investment homes throughout Florida. Based in Essex, FUSAD have over sixty UK homeowners on their books. Many of who have purchased their second or third investment home. One of the major reasons for their continued success has been that the Team focus in on what is important to the foreign investor who may be 4,500 miles away.

Dean Lacey-Freeman says "We offer a different service to most people selling real estate, we provide a hand-holding service giving support and guidance throughout the whole process. Furthermore, through our property management company based out in Florida, we see the whole project through. Our intention is to develop a long-term relationship with the client so that their investment is a success and they will go on to purchase another home through us".

FUSAD's origins date back to 1992 when they purchased their first home in Kissimmee, Florida. That soon became a success and they went on to buy further homes. The one thing that worries most potential purchasers is the fear that they will not be able to rent the property once they have bought it. That worry can now be dispelled through a guaranteed rental programme (available only through certain developers) which takes much of the risk out of the investment. Also with this rental programme it leaves the winter months free for you to either rent out or stay yourself and get away from the cold weather. FUSAD will help you apply for a visitors visa to allow you to stay in the States for up to 6 months of the year and this advice to homeowners is FREE.

Recent performances of stocks, shares and ISAS's have meant that many people have been looking round for other investment options and dozens of families have taken the view that 'bricks and mortar' are frequently the safest form of investment. A recent report published in the United States predicted that homes in Central Florida would appreciate by 72% over the next ten years. Florida is also a good option if you on have a small amount to invest, mortgages are available without any age qualification, our U.S. Licensed Mortgage Brokers will advise you further on that. The other 'non-quantifiable' benefit is the fun you get from owning a home in the vacation capital of the world. Not much enjoyment is gained from looking up share prices in the *Financial Times*, but a visit to Orlando brings a smile to all the family's faces, especially during winter.

FUSAD are a friendly company who believe passionately in Florida and many of them own homes themselves. By contacting them they are able to give you advice based on experience as homeowners and not just as a selling agency. The other benefit of using FUSAD is that there will be no forceful or pushy selling technique just good honest advice and support.

Buying abroad?

Don't let the currency markets blur your vision.

Halewood keep your dreams in focus.

Rapid movements in worldwide exchange rates can and frequently do change everything.

A European property costing £97,500 in October 2000 would have cost £110,475 by January 2001, an increase of over 10% in less than 4 months.

Halewood International Foreign Exchange have built up an enviable reputation by providing an unparalleled level of service to protect clients from foreign exchange risk and ensure substantial savings when buying currency for an overseas purchase.

"..dealing with HIFX felt almost too good to be true.. I feel that I have received a better service than outlined.." K. Byatt, Head Teacher

In a recent Reuters forex poll: Top 20 rankings for currency analysis, Halewood International was placed 2nd in the world.

Halewood International are now the UK's 10th fastest growing company.
[source Pricewaterhouse Coopers]

- **No Commission**
- **Free transfer of funds***
- **Commercial exchange rates**
- **Guaranteed forward prices**
- **Courteous, simple and cost effective service**
* One free telegraphic transfer or currency draft per transaction.

Halewood reduces the stress of buying abroad
For a free quotation or explanation of how our services could enhance your property purchase, please contact our Private Client Desk:

HALEWOOD
INTERNATIONAL
FOREIGN EXCHANGE

Tel +44(0)1753 859159
e-mail info@hifx.co.uk
www.hifx.co.uk

Federation of Overseas Property Developers, Agents and Consultants

Appendix V

Making it for Yourself: Business & Franchise Opportunities

The British Franchise Association
Thames View
Newtown Road
Henley-on-Thames
Oxon RG9 1HG
Tel: 01491 578049
www.british-franchise.org.uk

British Chambers of Commerce
Manning House
22 Carlisle Place
London SW1P
Tel: 020 7565 2000

Business Links
Tel: 0345 5677765 (signpost line)

Companies House
21 Bloomsbury Street
London WC1B
Tel: 0870 3333636
Web: www.companieshouse.gov.uk

Department of Trade & Industry
www.dti.gov.uk

*i*xtreme by Packard Bell

the computer that's full of surprises

Because intelligence means the ability to surprise, Packard Bell has designed the *i*xtreme 9200, a computer that turns your living room into a home cinema. With the latest in graphic card technology and a sound card with digital audio out, DVD, TV-out, Firewire ports for digital video and an Intel® Pentium® III processor, the *i*xtreme has a whole range of features to astonish you. And to help you take full advantage of the digital world, the *i*xtreme comes with Microsoft® Windows® Millennium Edition - the home version of the world's favourite software. *Available at Dixons, Currys and PC World stores. For more information please phone 01628 508222.*

because your computer should understand you.

vw.packardbell.co.uk

Packard Bell.

A division of NEC Computers International

Molly Maid

SUCCESS STORY

Wimbledon-based Molly Maid franchisee Sandra Redmond recently achieved third place and gained £2,000 prize money in the prestigious Franchisee of the Year Awards.

Congratulating Sandra on her success, Chief Executive of Molly Maid UK Pam Bader OBE FRSA said: "Success in Molly Maid depends upon two key factors. On one hand, the franchisee must be able to demonstrate a high standard of professionalism and gain and retain the confidence and trust of customers. On the other hand, the franchisee's personal qualities play a vital role in recruiting and retaining staff. Sandra's success is founded upon excellence in both these areas, together with general business management skills of a high order".

A key element in Sandra's success is the close attention she pays to maintaining quality standards and keeping in touch with her customers. This is reflected in the very high proportion of new business which comes from referrals by satisfied customers.

As her business has grown, Sandra has handed over much of the day-to-day administration of the business to a manager. This has enabled her to concentrate on strategic issues, particularly customer care and staff management. This policy is enabling her to implement plans for further expansion of the business.

Sandra has done much to enhance the standing of her business locally. As well as devoting energy and time to worthwhile community activities, she has also contributed much to local charities through various sponsorships.

Since the first Molly Maid UK franchise started in 1986, in Essex, the company has established franchises in most areas of the country. Over the last decade, expansion of the franchise network has taken place primarily in the south-east, particularly in the London area and Home Counties. Although opportunities in these areas are limited, there are still many franchise territories available elsewhere.

Main centres of population not yet reached by Molly Maid or which offer scope for additional franchises include Bournemouth, Brighton, Guildford and Swindon in the south, and Bath, Bristol, Cardiff, Cheltenham, Gloucester and Swansea in the south-west and Wales. In the midlands and East Anglia, opportunities exist in the Birmingham area, Cambridge, Coventry, Derby, Ipswich, Milton Keynes and Peterborough. Molly Maid is well-established in Scotland, but in northern England, franchise territories are still available in Liverpool, Manchester, Nottingham, Sheffield and Stoke-on-Trent.

People who are interested in starting a Molly Maid business can call Molly Maid UK on 0800 500950 to check out the potential in their area and obtain full details of the Molly Maid franchise opportunity.

8 November 2000

ever wanted...

...more time out of the office?

Working effectively can increase the bottom line of the organisation, reduce absenteeism and staff turnover by decreasing pressure at work - and give people more quality time for other activities.

Time/system A5 sized paper based planning systems are designed to keep diary details, project overviews, contact details and standard reference information all in one place - wherever you need them.

Time/system training and planning tools are designed to make individuals and organisations more effective. So, now you can work smarter - not harder giving you more time to play...

▣ Time/system®
And suddenly you have time

Inventorlink
5 Clipstone Street
London W1P 7EB
Tel: 020 73234323

National Federation of Enterprise Agencies
c/o NatWest Bank
Trinity Gardens
9-11 Bromham Road
Bedford MK40 2QU
Tel: 01234 354055

Patent Office
Tel: 0845 950 0505

Appendix VI

Private medical and health insurance

Abbey National Healthcare
Tel: 0800 222399

BUPA Healthcare
Tel: 0800 600 500

BCWA Healthcare
James Tudor House
90 Victoria Street
Bristol BS1 6DF
Tel: 0117 929 5555

Exeter Friendly Society
Lakeside House
Emporer Way
Exeter EX1 3FD
Tel: 08080 556 575

Legal & General Healthcare
Freepost
PO Box 2344
Hove
East Sussex BN3 1BR
Tel: 0500 669996

Norwich Union Healthcare Ltd
Chilworth House
Hampshire Corporate Park
Templars Way
Eastleigh
Hants SO5 3RY
Tel: 0800 300990

Nuffield Hospitals
Freephone: 0800 688 699

PPP Healthcare
Phillips House
Crescent Road
Tunbridge Wells,
Kent TN1 2PL
Tel: 0800 335 555

Royal Sun Alliance
Tamar House
St. Andrew's Cross
Plymouth PL1 1SG
Tel: 0800 300990

Standard Life Healthcare
Wey House
Farnham Road
Guilford
Surrey GU1 4XS
Tel: 01483 440550

Western Provident Association Ltd
Rivergate House
Blackbrook Park, Taunton
Somerset TA1 2PE
Tel: 01823 623 000

Appendix VII

Retirement

Retirement planning and advice

The Annuity Bureau
The Tower
11 York Road
London SE1 7NX
Tel: 020 7902 2300

DSS Pensions
Freepost BS5555/1
Bristol BS99 1BL
Pensions information line: 0845 731 3233

National Association of Citizens' Advice Bureau
115–123 Pentonville Road
London N1 9LZ
Tel: 020 7833 2181

Prudential Retirement Counselling Service
3rd Floor, Abbey Gate
57–75 Kings Rd.
Reading
Berks RG1 3AB
Tel: 0118 949 5808

Taxback Helpline
Tel: 0845 077 6543

Pensions

Regulators and further information:

OPAS: Occupational Pensions Advisory Service
11 Belgrave Road
London SW1V 1RB
Tel: 020 7233 8080

The Pensions Ombudsman
11 Belgrave Road
London
SW1V 1RB
Tel: 020 7834 9144

Pension Schemes Registry
PO Box 1NN
Newcastle-upon-Tyne
NE99 1NN
Tel: 0191 225 6393

Society of Pensions Consultants
St Bartholomew House
92 Fleet Street
London EC4Y 1DG
Tel: 020 7353 1688

War Pensions Agency
Norcross
Blackpool FY5 3WP
Tel: 01253 858 858
Fax: 01253 330 561

Providers:

Alliance Trust Savings Limited
PO Box 164 Meadow House
64 Reform Street
Dundee DD1 9YP
Tel: 01382 306006
Web: www.alliancetrusts.com

Allied Dunbar Assurance plc
9–15 Sackville Street
London W1X
Tel: 0207 434 3211

Direct Line
250 St. Vincent Street
Glasgow G2 5SH
Tel: 0845 3000 333

Direct Pensions Services Ltd
Freepost
19/21 Albion Place
Maidstone ME14 5BR
Tel: 0800 316 3050
Web: www.retire.uk.net

Eagle Star
1000 Parkway
Solent Business Park
Fareham PO15 7AA
Tel: 0800 363 422

Friends Provident
Pixam End
Dorking
Surrey RH4 1QA
Tel: 0870 608 3678
Web: www.friendsprovident.com

Halifax plc
Tel: 0845 605 5010
Web: www.halifax.co.uk

Legal & General
5th Floor Quadrant House
80-82 Regent Street
LondonW1R
Tel: 020 7734 3255

Lifestyle Financial Services
Socially Responsible Investment Centre
Fourteen Wright Street
Kingston upon Hull HU2 8HU
Tel: 0800 138 0851
Web: www.moneywells.co.uk

Marks & Spencer
Life & Pensions
Kings Meadow
Chester Business Park
Chester CH99 9LS
Tel: 0800 363 422

Pension Annuity Friendly Society Ltd
59–60 Mark Lane
London EC3R
Tel: 0207 680 8960

Swiss Life (UK)
103 Cannon Street
London EC4N
Tel: 0207 426 9400

Wesleyan Assurance Society
Colmore Circus
Birmingham B4 6AR
Tel: 0800 0 680 680
Web: www.wesleyan.co.uk

Appendix VIII

Funerals and Wills

Funeral plans and advice

Association of Burial Authorities
155 Upper Street
Islington
London N1 1RA
Tel: 020 7288 2522

Age Concern Funeral Plan
Freepost SEA3369
London SE21 8BR
Tel: 0800 387 718

Co-operative Funeral Bond
Co-operative Funeral Service
Freepost NW 3091A
Manchester M60 5SH
Tel: 0800 289 120

Dignity Funeral Plans
Freepost SEA0601
Sutton Coldfield
West Midlands B72 1BR
Tel: 0800 387 717

Federation of British Cremation Authorities
41 Salisbury Road
Carshalton
Surrey SM5 3HA
Tel: 020 8669 4521

Funeral Ombudsman Scheme
26–28 Bedford Row
London WC1 4HE
Tel: 020 7430 1112
Fax: 020 7430 1012

Funeral Planning Council
Melville House
70 Drymen Rd
Bearsden
Glasgow G61 2RP
Tel: 0141 942 5885
Fax: 0141 942 2323

Funeral Standards Council
30 North Road
Cardiff CF1 3DY
Tel: 029 2038 2046

Golden Charter
Tel: Funeral plans: 0800 833800

Help the Aged Funeral Plan
Tel: 0800 169 1112

Institute of Burial and Cremation Administration
Kelham Hall
Kelham
Nr Newark
Notts NG23 5QX
Tel/ Fax: 01636 708 311

National Association of Funeral Directors
618 Warwick Road
Solihull
West Midlands B91 1AA
Tel: 0121 709 0019

National Association of Pre-Paid Funeral Plans
618 Warwick Road
Solihull
West Midlands B91 1AA
Tel: 0121 711 1343
Fax: 0121 711 1351

The New Bereavement Benefits
Tel: 0845 731 3233

Wills and probate

Donor Development Dept
RNIB 224 Great Portland Street
London W1W 5AA
Tel: 0845 766 9999

Help the Aged
207–221 Pentonville Road
London N1 9UZ
Funeral Plan Tel: 0800 169 1112

The Law Society
113 Chancery Lane
London
WC2A 1PL
Tel: 020 7242 1222

The Law Society of Scotland
The Law Society's Hall
26 Drumsheugh Gardens
Edinburgh EH3 7YR
Tel: 0131 226 7411

The Law Society of Northern Ireland
Law Society House
98 Victoria Street
Belfast BT1 3JZ
Tel: 028 9023 1614

Legal Services Ombudsman
Sunlight House
Quay Street
Manchester M3 3JZ
Tel: 0161 839 7262

Office for the Supervision of Solicitors
Victoria Court
8 Dormer Place
Leamington Spa
CV32 5AE
Tel: 0845 608 6565

Probate Registry
Personal Applications Dept, 2nd Floor
Principal Registry, Family Division
Somerset House
Strand
London WC2R 1LP
Tel: 020 7936 6983 or 020 7936 6939

Index of Advertisers